COUNTY COUNCIL OF THE COUNTY OF LANARK
EDUCATION COMMITTEE

_____ School.

(1)   This book is the property of the Education Committee, and is intended for the use of scholars attending Schools in the County of Lanark

(2)   Parents and Guardians are asked to co-operate with the Teachers in seeing that the Book is kept clean and in good repair.

(3)   When a leaf becomes loose or gets torn, it should at once be shown to the Teacher of the class.

(4)   The Parent or Guardian of a scholar losing or mis-using a book will be required to replace it, or to refund to the Education Authority the value of the book.

(5)   The book must be covered by the pupil to whom it is issued.

Date	Name	Class

L.1247/O.M.

Touchstones 5

A TEACHING ANTHOLOGY

MICHAEL BENTON, M.A.
*Head of the English Department, Minchenden School,
Southgate*

PETER BENTON, M.A.
Head of English, The Grammar School, Letchworth

THE ENGLISH UNIVERSITIES PRESS LTD

ISBN 0 340 05234 1

First Published 1971

Copyright © 1971 M. G. Benton and P. Benton

The English Universities Press Ltd
St Paul's House, Warwick Lane, London EC4P 4AH

PRINTED AND BOUND IN GREAT BRITAIN BY
HAZELL WATSON AND VINEY LTD
AYLESBURY, BUCKS

Contents

iii

iv

v

vii

To the Teacher

In Book 4 we concluded the teaching sections which have been an integral part of all the earlier books in the series and, with this exception, Book 5, the final *Touchstones* volume, retains the pattern of its predecessors. We have, however, increased the number of poems, pictures and creative writing suggestions. This last section is now Discussion and Writing and we have attempted where possible to raise questions of importance and indicate ways of initiating discussion as well as to suggest openings for pupils' own original writing.

We have grouped the material so that the teacher will be able to deal with several poems, linked by some common quality of technique, subject matter, style or attitude, in any one lesson or sequence of lessons. Whenever a strong conflict arises between the attitudes of poets, we have tried to bring this out and frequently use it as a starting point in the Discussion and Writing pages which appear at the end of each section. There is, in addition, a new departure in this volume with the inclusion of a section of Poems to Compare where pairs of poems on related themes are presented. We suggest that it may be useful to split classes into smaller groups for the purpose of discussing these poems – and indeed it is a method that works well with most other poems in the book.

Whilst it is possible to use *Touchstones 5* simply as a collection of one hundred and sixty poems and ignore the suggestions for original writing, treating the photographs and pictures as illustrations, we hope that few teachers will do so. We regard it as essential that pupils should not only read poetry but try to write their own and come to grips with their own feelings and experience in this way. The pictures are not merely decorative but are an important part of the text and are all linked to the Discussion and Writing sections. Many of the photographs are by major international photographers such as Bill Brandt, Henri Cartier-Bresson and Marc Riboud and there is, as usual, a range of reproductions of painting and sculpture by famous artists. We have tried throughout to find pictures which are, above all, relevant both to the poems and to adolescent experience, interests and imagination.

Although we do suggest certain lines of thought we do not wish the book to be followed from cover to cover as a 'course', and we hope that the teacher will find sufficient flexibility in the arrangement to be able to select and modify the material according to his own tastes and the abilities and interests of his pupils.

Creative Writing

There are many ways of stimulating children's writing and every teacher has his own methods. We consider that it would be presumptuous to give too much direction and we have, in the main, limited ourselves to suggestions in the creative writing sections. However, we do feel that rather different emphases are needed in the later years: the moodiness and unpredictability which indicate the emotional changes going on in many adolescent children are familiar to all teachers. In the creative writing sections, as in the anthology, we have aimed at providing material which in several ways will help teenagers to cope with their own growing-up. First, we have made use of their increasing awareness of themselves by inviting them to write poems which require them to sort out their own feelings and attitudes towards experience. Secondly, we have suggested topics for discussion and writing which give children the chance either to show a wider social awareness or to come to terms with more complicated ideas and feelings; the sections on love and war, for instance, should help here. Thirdly, while we would still encourage pupils to write free verse, it is our experience that older children often like the discipline of writing in regular patterns. Using the form of some of the poems we anthologise affords *some* children the satisfaction of having a recognisable pattern of words at which to aim. The manipulation of rhymes, syllables and metres can help them to define the boundaries of their poems and gives direction to their ideas without necessarily sacrificing the original spontaneity and feeling. For others, however, anything more structured than a seventeen syllable haiku proves inhibiting; but, whatever the reaction of the individual pupil to writing in a particular form, there is no doubt that some appreciation of the difficulties of writing in regular patterns is gained and this, in turn, helps the pupil to enjoy poetry more fully as well as become more discriminating in his reading.

The suggested approaches to creative writing are all ones which we have found successful. If teachers wish to pursue the subject of children's writing further, we would recommend the following books: Ted Hughes, *Poetry in the Making,* Chapters One to Five (Faber); Robert Druce, *The Eye of Innocence* (University of London Press); Brian Powell, *English Through Poetry Writing* (Heinemann); and M. Langdon, *Let the Children Write: An Explanation of Intensive Writing* (Longmans). We have found pictures and photographs invaluable as 'starters', particularly in that they focus attention on detail and help children to *see* as well as to look. We hope that teachers will also use other stimuli – e.g. music, or objects brought in by pupils and teacher – when appropriate. We have already dealt with this topic at greater length in the introductions to earlier books in the series.

A final word: poems cannot be written on demand and we would emphasise that in using the Discussion and Writing sections teachers should encourage the class to talk around our suggestions and not present these as 'exercises' which must be completed. Our own open-ended questions in these sections are not meant in any way to dictate the nature of the pupil's response: they provide stimuli which the pupil should feel free to ignore if he so chooses, or to adapt in the light of his own experience.

M. G. B.
P. B.

DAYS

Days

What are days for?
Days are where we live.
They come, they wake us
Time and time over.
They are to be happy in:
Where can we live but days?
Ah, solving that question
Brings the priest and the doctor
In their long coats
Running over the fields.

PHILIP LARKIN

What is our Life?

What is our life? A play of passion.
And what our mirth but music of division?
Our mothers' wombs the tiring houses be
Where we are dressed for this short comedy.
Heaven the judicious sharp spectator is
Who sits and marks what here we do amiss.
The graves that hide us from the searching sun
Are like drawn curtains when the play is done.
Thus playing post we to our latest rest,
And then we die in earnest, not in jest.

SIR WALTER RALEIGH

One Evening

As I walked out one evening,
   Walking down Bristol Street,
The crowds upon the pavement
   Were fields of harvest wheat.

And down by the brimming river
   I heard a lover sing
Under an arch of the railway:
   'Love has no ending.

I'll love you, dear, I'll love you
   Till China and Africa meet,
And the river jumps over the mountain
   And the salmon sing in the street.

I'll love you till the ocean
   Is folded and hung up to dry,
And the seven stars go squawking
   Like geese about the sky.

The years shall run like rabbits,
   For in my arms I hold
The Flower of the Ages,
   And the first love of the world.'

But all the clocks in the city
   Began to whirr and chime:
'O let not Time deceive you,
   You cannot conquer Time.

'In the burrows of the Nightmare
   Where Justice naked is,
Time watches from the shadow
   And coughs when you would kiss.

'In headaches and in worry
  Vaguely life leaks away,
And Time will have his fancy
  To-morrow or to-day.

'Into many a green valley
  Drifts the appalling snow;
Time breaks the threaded dances
  And the diver's brilliant bow.

'O plunge your hands in water,
  Plunge them in up to the wrist;
Stare, stare in the basin
  And wonder what you've missed.

'The glacier knocks in the cupboard,
  The desert sighs in the bed,
And the crack in the tea-cup opens
  A lane to the land of the dead.

'Where the beggars raffle the banknotes
  And the Giant is enchanting to Jack,
And the Lily-white Boy is a Roarer,
  And Jill goes down on her back.

'O look, look in the mirror,
  O look in your distress;
Life remains a blessing
  Although you cannot bless.

'O stand, stand at the window
  As the tears scald and start;
You shall love your crooked neighbour
  With your crooked heart'.

It was late, late in the evening
  The lovers they were gone;
The clocks had ceased their chiming,
  And the deep river ran on.

W. H. AUDEN

3

'I Look Into My Glass'

I look into my glass,
And view my wasting skin,
And say, 'Would God it came to pass
My heart had shrunk as thin!'

For then, I, undistrest
By hearts grown cold to me,
Could lonely wait my endless rest
With equanimity.

But Time, to make me grieve,
Part steals, lets part abide;
And shakes this fragile frame at eve
With throbbings of noontide.

THOMAS HARDY

During Wind and Rain

They sing their dearest songs –
He, she, all of them – yea,
Treble and tenor and bass,
   And one to play;
With the candles mooning each face. . . .
   Ah, no; the years O!
How the sick leaves reel down in throngs!

They clear the creeping moss –
Elders and juniors – aye,
Making the pathways neat
   And the garden gay;
And they build a shady seat. . . .
   Ah, no; the years, the years;
See, the white storm-birds wing across!

They are blithely breakfasting all –
Men and maidens – yea,
Under the summer tree,
   With a glimpse of the bay,
While pet fowl come to the knee. . . .
   Ah, no; the years O!
And the rotten rose is ript from the wall.

They change to a high new house,
He, she, all of them – aye,
Clocks and carpets and chairs
   On the lawn all day,
And brightest things that are theirs. . . .
   Ah, no; the years, the years;
Down their carved names the rain-drop ploughs.

THOMAS HARDY

Wants

Beyond all this, the wish to be alone :
However the sky grows dark with invitation-cards
However we follow the printed directions of sex
However the family is photographed under the flagstaff –
Beyond all this, the wish to be alone.

Beneath it all, desire of oblivion runs :
Despite the artful tensions of the calendar,
The life insurance, the tabled fertility rites,
The costly aversion of the eyes from death –
Beneath it all, desire of oblivion runs.

PHILIP LARKIN

Death on a Live Wire

Treading a field I saw afar
A laughing fellow climbing the cage
That held the grinning tensions of wire,
Alone, and no girl gave him courage.

Up he climbed on the diamond struts,
Diamond cut diamond, till he stood
With the insulators brooding like owls
And all their live wisdom if he would.

I called to him climbing and asked him to say
What thrust him into the singeing sky :
The one word he told me the wind took away,
So I shouted again, but the wind passed me by

And the gust of his answer tore at his coat
And stuck him stark on the lightning's bough;
Humanity screeched in his manacled throat
And he cracked with flame like a figure of straw.

6

Turning, burning, he dangled black,
A hot sun swallowing at his fork
And shaking embers out of his back,
Planting his shadow of fear in the chalk.

O then he danced an incredible dance
With soot in his sockets, hanging at heels;
Uprooted mandrakes screamed in his loins,
His legs thrashed and lashed like electric eels;

For now he embraced the talent of iron,
The white-hot ore that comes from the hill,
The Word out of which the electrons run,
The snake in the rod and the miracle;

And as he embraced it the girders turned black,
Fused metal wept and great tears ran down
Till his fingers like snails at last came unstuck
And he fell through the cage of the sun.

MICHAEL BALDWIN

'Out, Out—'

The buzz saw snarled and rattled in the yard
And made dust and dropped stove-length sticks of wood,
Sweet-scented stuff when the breeze drew across it.
And from there those that lifted eyes could count
Five mountain ranges one behind the other
Under the sunset far into Vermont.
And the saw snarled and rattled, snarled and rattled,
As it ran light, or had to bear a load.
And nothing happened: day was all but done.
Call it a day, I wish they might have said
To please the boy by giving him the half hour
That a boy counts so much when saved from work.
His sister stood beside them in her apron
To tell them 'Supper'. At the word, the saw,
As if to prove saws knew what supper meant,
Leaped out at the boy's hand, or seemed to leap –
He must have given the hand. However it was,
Neither refused the meeting. But the hand!
The boy's first outcry was a rueful laugh,
As he swung toward them holding up the hand
Half in appeal, but half as if to keep
The life from spilling. Then the boy saw all –
Since he was old enough to know, big boy
Doing a man's work, though a child at heart –
He saw all spoiled. 'Don't let him cut my hand off –
The doctor, when he comes. Don't let him sister!'
So. But the hand was gone already.
The doctor put him in the dark of ether.
He lay and puffed his lips out with his breath.
And then – the watcher at his pulse took fright.
No one believed. They listened at his heart.
Little – less – nothing! – and that ended it.
No more to build on there. And they, since they
Were not the one dead, turned to their affairs.

ROBERT FROST

8

Mid-Term Break

I sat all morning in the college sick bay
Counting bells knelling classes to a close.
At two o'clock our neighbours drove me home.

In the porch I met my father crying –
He had always taken funerals in his stride –
And Big Jim Evans saying it was a hard blow.

The baby cooed and laughed and rocked the pram
When I came in, and I was embarrassed
By old men standing up to shake my hand

And tell me they were 'sorry for my trouble',
Whispers informed strangers I was the eldest,
Away at school, as my mother held my hand

In hers and coughed out angry tearless sighs.
At ten o'clock the ambulance arrived
With the corpse, stanched and bandaged by the nurses.

Next morning I went up into the room. Snowdrops
And candles soothed the bedside; I saw him
For the first time in six weeks. Paler now,

Wearing a poppy bruise on his left temple,
He lay in the four foot box as in his cot.
No gaudy scars, the bumper knocked him clear.

A four foot box, a foot for every year.

SEAMUS HEANEY

At The Florist's

A man enters a florist's
and chooses some flowers
the florist wraps up the flowers
the man puts his hand in his pocket
to find the money
the money to pay for the flowers
but at the same time he puts
all of a sudden
his hand on his heart
and he falls

At the same time that he falls
the money rolls on the floor
and then the flowers fall
at the same time as the man
at the same time as the money
and the florist stands there
with the money rolling
with the flowers spoiling
with the man dying
obviously this is very sad
and she's got to do something
the florist
but she doesn't know quite where to start
she doesn't know
at which end to begin

There's so many things to do
with this man dying
with these flowers spoiling
and this money
this money that rolls
that doesn't stop rolling.

JACQUES PRÉVERT
(trans. L. Ferlinghetti)

'Death and the miser', *Hieronymus Bosch*

Do Not Go Gentle Into That Good Night

Do not go gentle into that good night,
Old age should burn and rave at close of day;
Rage, rage against the dying of the light.

Though wise men at their end know dark is right,
Because their words had forked no lightning they
Do not go gentle into that good night.

Good men, the last wave by, crying how bright
Their frail deeds might have danced in a green bay,
Rage, rage against the dying of the light.

Wild men who caught and sang the sun in flight,
And learn, too late, they grieved it on its way,
Do not go gentle into that good night.

Grave men, near death, who see with blinding sight
Blind eyes could blaze like meteors and be gay,
Rage, rage against the dying of the light.

And you, my father, there on the sad height,
Curse, bless, me now with your fierce tears, I pray.
Do not go gentle into that good night.
Rage, rage against the dying of the light.

DYLAN THOMAS

Because I Could Not Stop for Death

Because I could not stop for Death –
He kindly stopped for me –
The Carriage held but just Ourselves –
And Immortality.

We slowly drove – He knew no haste
And I had put away
My labor and my leisure too,
For His Civility –

We passed the School, where Children strove
At Recess – in the Ring –
We passed the Fields of Gazing Grain –
We passed the Setting Sun –

Or rather – He passed Us –
The Dews drew quivering and chill –
For only Gossamer, my Gown –
My Tippet – only Tulle –

We paused before a House that seemed
A Swelling of the Ground –
A Roof was scarcely visible –
The Cornice – in the Ground –

Since then – 'tis Centuries – and yet
Feels shorter than the Day
I first surmised the Horses' Heads
Were toward Eternity –

EMILY DICKINSON

'Knight, death and the devil', *Dürer*

Death Be Not Proud

Death be not proud, though some have called thee
Mighty and dreadful, for, thou art not soe,
For, those, whom thou think'st, thou dost overthrow,
Die not, poore death, nor yet canst thou kill mee;
From rest and sleepe, which but thy pictures bee,
Much pleasure, then from thee, much more must flow,
And soonest our best men with thee doe goe,
Rest of their bones, and soules deliverie.
Thou art slave to Fate, chance, kings, and desperate men,
And dost with poyson, warre, and sicknesse dwell,
And poppie, or charmes can make us sleepe as well,
And better than thy stroake; why swell'st thou then?
One short sleepe past, wee wake eternally,
And death shall be no more, Death thou shalt die.

JOHN DONNE

Sonnet 71

No longer mourn for me when I am dead
Than you shall hear the surly sullen bell
Give warning to the world that I am fled
From this vile world, with vilest worms to dwell:
Nay, if you read this line, remember not
The hand that writ it; for I love you so,
That I in your sweet thoughts would be forgot,
If thinking on me then should make you woe.
O, if, I say, you look upon this verse
When I perhaps compounded am with clay,
Do not so much as my poor name rehearse,
But let your love even with my life decay;
　　Lest the wise world should look into your moan,
　　And mock you with me after I am gone.

WILLIAM SHAKESPEARE

5 Ways to Kill a Man

There are many cumbersome ways to kill a man:
you can make him carry a plank of wood
to the top of a hill and nail him to it. To do this
properly you require a crowd of people
wearing sandals, a cock that crows, a cloak
to dissect, a sponge, some vinegar and one
man to hammer the nails home.

Or you can take a length of steel,
shaped and chased in a traditional way,
and attempt to pierce the metal cage he wears.
But for this you need white horses,
English trees, men with bows and arrows,
at least two flags, a prince and a
castle to hold your banquet in.

Dispensing with nobility, you may, if the wind
allows, blow gas at him. But then you need
a mile of mud sliced through with ditches,
not to mention black boots, bomb craters,
more mud, a plague of rats, a dozen songs
and some round hats made of steel.

In an age of aeroplanes, you may fly
miles above your victim and dispose of him by
pressing one small switch. All you then
require is an ocean to separate you, two
systems of government, a nation's scientists,
several factories, a psychopath and
land that no one needs for several years.

These are, as I began, cumbersome ways
to kill a man. Simpler, direct, and much more neat
is to see that he is living somewhere in the middle
of the twentieth century, and leave him there.

EDWIN BROCK

Fire and Ice

Some say the world will end in fire,
Some say in ice.
From what I've tasted of desire
I hold with those who favour fire.
But if it had to perish twice,
I think I know enough of hate
To say that for destruction ice
Is also great
And would suffice.

ROBERT FROST

Discussion and Writing

1 Several of the poems in this section ask the question posed by Sir
  Walter Raleigh, *What is our Life?* (p. 1), and attempt to come
  to terms with the mystery of human existence.
    What do *you* make of the fact that millions of creatures called
  homo sapiens are born, live for seventy-odd years on a lump of
  rock travelling round the sun, and then decay, die and become
  dust? Ask yourself Raleigh's question and try to find appropriate
  words and metaphors to answer it for yourself in a poem.
2 Look at Robert Frost's *Fire and Ice* (or the pair of poems on pp.
  188 and 189). How do you visualise the end of the world? Try to
  write a poem about it.
3 Pages 6 to 17 contain a number of poems and two pictures all
  of which are concerned with the subject of death. Some of the
  poems are narratives, like '*Out, Out—*' (p. 8) or *Mid-Term Break*
  (p. 9) where, through elaborating a particular incident, the writer
  dramatises death and its effects before us; other poems are made
  up of a series of images through which the poet tries to visualise
  death for us – *Because I could not stop for Death* (p. 13) works
  in this way, as, indeed, do the two pictures.

17

If you ask the class how many people have actually seen a dead person you will possibly be surprised at the small number, yet it is a subject which people constantly write and talk about. How do *you* imagine death? After discussing the poems and pictures mentioned above you may be able to write something connected with the idea of death, perhaps developed around an incident or a series of images.

4 The title poem to this section, Philip Larkin's *Days* on p. 1, may well puzzle you in that the question at the end of the first verse is answered only obliquely in the second. What is the main idea which the poem expresses?

You could use this short poem as a model, or try to write a 17 syllable haiku, and concentrate on simply capturing *a single idea* in as few words as possible connected with the theme of time, mortality and death.

5 If you or your parents have a family photograph album, you may find that looking through it gives rise to many curious sensations. Did I really look like that? Is that really me? Is there any link between that baby in the picture and the teenager I am now? And did my parents look and dress like that? It is worth trying the experiment and you will probably find some ideas for a piece of original writing here.

6 Closely linked with the idea of looking back which is mentioned above, is the question of how you see yourself in the future.

Can you project yourself ten, twenty . . . fifty years into the future and imagine what you will be like then? Perhaps you could describe your imagined self as another might see you.

PEOPLE AND PLACES

In The Snack-Bar

A cup capsizes along the formica,
slithering with a dull clatter.
A few heads turn in the crowded evening snack-bar.
An old man is trying to get to his feet
from the low round stool fixed to the floor.
Slowly he levers himself up, his hands have no power.
He is up as far as he can get. The dismal hump
looming over him forces his head down.
He stands in his stained beltless gaberdine
like a monstrous animal caught in a tent
in some story. He sways slightly,
the face not seen, bent down
in shadow under his cap.
Even on his feet he is staring at the floor
or would be, if he could see.
I notice now his stick, once painted white
but scuffed and muddy, hanging from his right arm.
Long-blind, hunchback born, half paralysed
he stands
fumbling with the stick
and speaks:
'I want – to go to the – toilet.'

It is down two flights of stairs, but we go.
I take his arm. 'Give me – your arm – it's better,' he says.
Inch by inch we drift towards the stairs.
A few yards of floor are like a landscape
to be negotiated, in the slow setting out
time has almost stopped. I concentrate
my life to his: crunch of spilt sugar,

slidy puddle from the night's umbrellas,
table edges, people's feet,
hiss of the coffee-machine, voices and laughter,
smell of cigar, hamburgers, wet coats steaming,
and the slow dangerous inches to the stairs.
I put his right hand on the rail
and take his stick. He clings to me. The stick
is in his left hand, probing the treads.
I guide his arm and tell him the steps.
And slowly we go down. And slowly we go down.
White tiles and mirrors at last. He shambles
uncouth into the clinical gleam.
I set him in position, stand behind him
and wait with his stick.
His brooding reflection darkens the mirror
but the trickle of his water is thin and slow,
an old man's apology for living.
Painful ages to close his trousers and coat –
I do up the last buttons for him.
He asks doubtfully, 'Can I – wash my hands?'
I fill the basin, clasp his soft fingers round the soap.
He washes, feebly, patiently. There is no towel.
I press the pedal of the drier, draw his hands
gently into the roar of the hot air.
But he cannot rub them together,
drags out a handkerchief to finish.
He is glad to leave the contraption, and face the stairs.
He climbs, and steadily enough.
He climbs, we climb. He climbs
with many pauses but with that one
persisting patience of the undefeated
which is the nature of man when all is said.
And slowly we go up. And slowly we go up.
The faltering, unfaltering steps
take him at last to the door
across that endless, yet not endless waste of floor.
I watch him helped on a bus. It shudders off in the rain.
The conductor bends to hear where he wants to go.

Gipsy boys. *Photo: Robert Smithies*

Wherever he could go it would be dark
and yet he must trust men.
Without embarrassment or shame
he must announce his most pitiful needs
in a public place. No one sees his face.
Does he know how frightening he is in his strangeness
under his mountainous coat, his hands like wet leaves
stuck to the half-white stick?
His life depends on many who would evade him.
But he cannot reckon up the chances,
having one thing to do,
to haul his blind hump through these rains of August.
Dear Christ, to be born for this!

EDWIN MORGAN

Poem in October

It was my thirtieth year to heaven
Woke to my hearing from harbour and neighbour wood
And the mussel pooled and the heron
Priested shore
The morning beckon
With water praying and call of seagull and rook
And the knock of sailing boats on the net webbed wall
Myself to set foot
That second
In the still sleeping town and set forth.

My birthday began with the water-
Birds and the birds of the winged trees flying my name
Above the farms and the white horses
And I rose
In rainy autumn
And walked abroad in a shower of all my days.

High tide and the heron dived when I took the road
Over the border
And the gates
Of the town closed as the town awoke.

A springful of larks in a rolling
Cloud and the roadside bushes brimming with whistling
Blackbirds and the sun of October
Summery
On the hill's shoulder,
Here were fond climates and sweet singers suddenly
Come in the morning where I wandered and listened
To the rain wringing
Wind blow cold
In the wood faraway under me.

Pale rain over the dwindling harbour
And over the sea wet church the size of a snail
With its horns through mist and the castle
Brown as owls
But all the gardens
Of spring and summer were blooming in the tall tales
Beyond the border and under the lark full cloud.
There could I marvel
My birthday
Away but the weather turned around.

It turned away from the blithe country
And down the other air and the blue altered sky
Streamed again a wonder of summer
With apples
Pears and red currants
And I saw in the turning so clearly a child's
Forgotten mornings when he walked with his mother
Through the parables
Of sun light
And the legends of the green chapels

And the twice told fields of infancy
That his tears burned my cheeks and his heart moved in
    mine.
These were the woods the river and sea
    Where a boy
    In the listening
Summertime of the dead whispered the truth of his joy
To the trees and the stones and the fish in the tide.
    And the mystery
    Sang alive
Still in the water and singingbirds.

    And there could I marvel my birthday
Away but the weather turned around. And the true
    Joy of the long dead child sang burning
    In the sun.
    It was my thirtieth
Year to heaven stood there then in the summer noon
Though the town below lay leaved with October blood.
    O may my heart's truth
    Still be sung
On this high hill in a year's turning.

DYLAN THOMAS

Mr Bleaney

'This was Mr. Bleaney's room. He stayed
The whole time he was at the Bodies, till
They moved him.' Flowered curtains, thin and frayed,
Fall to within five inches of the sill,

Whose window shows a strip of building land,
Tussocky, littered. 'Mr. Bleaney took
My bit of garden properly in hand.'
Bed, upright chair, sixty-watt bulb, no hook

Behind the door, no room for books or bags –
'I'll take it.' So it happens that I lie
Where Mr. Bleaney lay, and stub my fags
On the same saucer-souvenir, and try

Stuffing my ears with cotton-wool, to drown
The jabbering set he egged her on to buy.
I know his habits – what time he came down,
His preference for sauce to gravy, why

He kept on plugging at the four aways –
Likewise their yearly frame : the Frinton folk
Who put him up for summer holidays,
And Christmas at his sister's house in Stoke.

But if he stood and watched the frigid wind
Tousling the clouds, lay on the fusty bed
Telling himself that this was home, and grinned,
And shivered, without shaking off the dread

That how we live measures our own nature,
And at his age having no more to show
Than one hired box should make him pretty sure
He warranted no better, I don't know.

PHILIP LARKIN

Out of Countenance

Give oneself a face
With the deployed cigarette,
The distrait
Glasses of the dark,
A tan, the fisted pipe's clenched grin,
Make-up's open mask
Or the separating bridge
Of a frank smile.

Put up the defences
Like sincere fans,
Fingers disposed,
Dropped curtain of hair
On bearded eyebrows
Lowered like a blind.
Or grip the nose
In a quiet think.

Masquers all, we ply
Self's harlequin trade.
The spangled eyelids
Wink their flash
Intelligence, but only
When the eyes are shut.
Our one hope, that watchers gaze
Behind, not through the masks we choose.

JAMES KIRKUP

The Clown III

Others are noble and admired –
The ones who walk the tightrope without nets,
The one who goes inside the lion's cage,
And all the grave, audacious acrobats.
Away from fear and rage
He simply is the interval for tired

People who cannot bear
Too much excitement. They can see in him
Their own lost innocence or else their fear
(For him no metal bars or broken limb).
Have they forgotten that it takes as much
Boldness to tumble, entertain and jest
When loneliness walks tightropes in your breast
And every joke is like a wild beast's touch?

ELIZABETH JENNINGS

'The circus', *Seurat*

The Folk Singers

Re-turning time-turned words,
Fitting each weathered song
To a new-grooved harmony,
They pluck slick strings and swing
A sad heart's equilibrium.

Numb passion, pearled in the shy
Shell of a country love
And strung on a frail tune,
Looks sharp now, strikes a pose
Like any rustic new to the bright town.

Their pre-packed take will sell
Ten thousand times: pale love
Rouged for the streets. Humming
Solders all broken hearts. Death's edge
Blunts on the narcotic strumming.

SEAMUS HEANEY

Not Waving But Drowning

Nobody heard him, the dead man,
But still he lay moaning:
I was much further out than you thought
And not waving but drowning.

Poor chap, he always loved larking
And now he's dead
It must have been too cold for him his heart gave way,
They said.

Oh, no no no no, it was too cold always
(Still the dead one lay moaning)
I was much too far out all my life
And not waving but drowning.

STEVIE SMITH

28

Portrait of a young girl, Eaton Place. *Photo: Bill Brandt*

The Unknown Citizen

He was found by the Bureau of Statistics to be
One against whom there was no official complaint,
And all the reports on his conduct agree
That, in the modern sense of an old-fashioned word, he was
    a saint,
For in everything he did he served the Greater Community.
Except for the war till the day he retired
He worked in a factory and never got fired.
But satisfied his employers, Fudge Motors Inc.
Yet he wasn't a scab or odd in his views,
For his Union reports that he paid his dues,
(Our report on his Union shows it was sound)
And our Social Psychology workers found
That he was popular with his mates and liked a drink.
The Press are convinced that he bought a paper every day
And that his reactions to advertisements were normal in
    every way.
Policies taken out in his name prove that he was fully insured,
And his Health-card shows he was once in hospital but left it
    cured.
Both Producers Research and High-Grade Living declare
He was fully sensible to the advantages of the Instalment Plan
And had everything necessary to the Modern Man,
A phonograph, a radio, a car and a frigidaire.
Our researchers into Public Opinion are content
That he held the proper opinions for the time of year;
When there was peace, he was for peace; when there was war,
    he went.
He was married and added five children to the population,
Which our Eugenist says was the right number for a parent of
    his generation,
And our teachers report that he never interfered with their
    education.
Was he free? Was he happy? The question is absurd;
Had anything been wrong, we should certainly have heard.

W. H. AUDEN

The Whitsun Weddings

That Whitsun, I was late getting away :
    Not till about
One-twenty on the sunlit Saturday
Did my three-quarters-empty train pull out,
All windows down, all cushions hot, all sense
Of being in a hurry gone. We ran
Behind the backs of houses, crossed a street
Of blinding windscreens, smelt the fish-dock; thence
The river's level drifting breadth began,
Where sky and Lincolnshire and water meet.

All afternoon, through the tall heat that slept
    For miles inland,
A slow and stopping curve southwards we kept.
Wide farms went by, short-shadowed cattle, and
Canals with floatings of industrial froth;
A hothouse flashed uniquely : hedges dipped
And rose : and now and then a smell of grass
Displaced the reek of buttoned carriage-cloth
Until the next town, new and nondescript,
Approached with acres of dismantled cars.

At first, I didn't notice what a noise
    The weddings made
Each station that we stopped at : sun destroys
The interest of what's happening in the shade,
And down the long cool platforms whoops and skirls
I took for porters larking with the mails,
And went on reading. Once we started, though,
We passed them, grinning and pomaded, girls
In parodies of fashion, heels and veils,
All posed irresolutely, watching us go,

As if out on the end of an event
　　　Waving goodbye
To something that survived it. Struck, I leant
More promptly out next time, more curiously,
And saw it all again in different terms :
The fathers with broad belts under their suits
And seamy foreheads; mothers loud and fat;
An uncle shouting smut; and then the perms,
The nylon gloves and jewellery-substitutes,
The lemons, mauves, and olive-ochres that

Marked off the girls unreally from the rest.
　　　Yes, from cafés
And banquet-halls up yards, and bunting-dressed
Coach-party annexes, the wedding-days
Were coming to an end. All down the line
Fresh couples climbed aboard : the rest stood round;
The last confetti and advice were thrown,
And, as we moved, each face seemed to define
Just what it saw departing : children frowned
At something dull; fathers had never known

Success so huge and wholly farcical;
　　　The women shared
The secret like a happy funeral;
While girls, gripping their handbags tighter, stared
At a religious wounding. Free at last,
And loaded with the sum of all they saw,
We hurried towards London, shuffling gouts of steam.
Now fields were building-plots, and poplars cast
Long shadows over major roads, and for
Some fifty minutes, that in time would seem

Just long enough to settle hats and say
　　　I nearly died,
A dozen marriages got under way.
They watched the landscape, sitting side by side
– An Odeon went past, a cooling tower,

And someone running up to bowl – and none
Thought of the others they would never meet
Or how their lives would all contain this hour.
I thought of London spread out in the sun,
Its postal districts packed like squares of wheat:

There we were aimed. And as we raced across
      Bright knots of rail
Past standing Pullmans, walls of blackened moss
Came close, and it was nearly done, this frail
Travelling coincidence; and what it held
Stood ready to be loosed with all the power
That being changed can give. We slowed again,
And as the tightened brakes took hold, there swelled
A sense of falling, like an arrow-shower
Sent out of sight, somewhere becoming rain.

PHILIP LARKIN

After Apple-Picking

My long two-pointed ladder's sticking through a tree
Toward heaven still,
And there's a barrel that I didn't fill
Beside it, and there may be two or three
Apples I didn't pick upon some bough.
But I am done with apple-picking now.
Essence of winter sleep is on the night,
The scent of apples : I am drowsing off.
I cannot rub the strangeness from my sight
I got from looking through a pane of glass
I skimmed this morning from the drinking trough
And held against the world of hoary grass.
It melted, and I let it fall and break.
But I was well
Upon my way to sleep before it fell,
And I could tell
What form my dreaming was about to take
Magnified apples appear and disappear,

Stem end and blossom end,
And every fleck of russet showing clear.
My instep arch not only keeps the ache,
It keeps the pressure of a ladder-round.
I feel the ladder sway as the boughs bend.
And I keep hearing from the cellar bin
The rumbling sound
Of load on load of apples coming in.
For I have had too much
Of apple-picking: I am overtired
Of the great harvest I myself desired.
There were ten thousand thousand fruit to touch,
Cherish in hand, lift down, and not let fall.
For all
That struck the earth,
No matter if not bruised or spiked with stubble,
Went sure to the cider-apple heap
As of no worth.
One can see what will trouble
This sleep of mine, whatever sleep it is.
Were he not gone,
The woodchuck could say whether it's like his
Long sleep, as I describe its coming on,
Or just some human sleep.

ROBERT FROST

Discussion and Writing

1 Nobody likes being shut in, confined to a small space and for most
people it would be intolerable to be in this situation for a lengthy
period. Think about what your feelings would be and what ten-
sions you might expect to feel build up in yourself if you were in
such a situation. What sort of details might you notice if you were
imprisoned in a small cell, potholing through foot-high passages
with a mountain pressing down above you, or in the confined space
of a submarine or space-craft? Perhaps you could write about one
of these subjects or something similar.

2 Think back to your very earliest memories and try, with others of your group, to establish exactly what these were and how old you were. They might perhaps be very important or dramatic but they are likely to be quite trivial incidents. There might be an idea for a poem here.

3 Think about the place you live in – perhaps a suburban street, a block of flats, a terrace, a council estate, or a more isolated situation. What seems to you to be its essential character and what makes it like that? How do you feel about it? Are you very much attached to it or do you dislike it? Are you indifferent? Try to convey the idea of your street and what you feel about it in a piece of original writing. Remember, it is the tiny details that only you know that will make a real and vivid picture.

4 Parks usually have a character of their own. Some are neat and formal, with carefully laid out walks, others are places where football is played and are closer to recreation grounds, yet others are full of swings and paddling pools, boating lakes and ice-cream sellers, bandstands and crowds and litter. Perhaps you could write a poem about a local park you know well.

5 Wherever you live yourself you probably feel that certain types of environment are not for you. How do you react to the idea of:

Living in a suburban house with a garden full of gnomes and plaster toadstools?

Living on the fifteenth floor of a block of system built flats in the heart of an industrial city?

Living in a tiny back to back terrace house with four rooms?

Living over a shop in a shopping centre?

Perhaps you could imagine what life might be like in a different environment and write about it.

6 Many of you will have visited a circus though probably not recently. Although Seurat painted his circus picture, reproduced on p. 27, in 1890, and circuses have changed in many ways, it still seems to capture much of the elusive magic of this form of entertainment. It is worth looking carefully at the picture and discussing it in some detail before trying to write either about what you see there, or a related topic.

7 The photograph on p. 21 shows two 14-year-old Gipsy boys in a café. Look at the picture carefully. What details of their dress and manner strike you? What is your immediate response to the picture? Perhaps you could write a portrait of them in words.

Solar eclipse. *Photo: Dr G. A. Newkirk, Jr.*

8 The picture above shows an eclipse of the sun in May 1970 at the point when the main body of the sun is hidden behind the moon and all that can be seen of it is the flaring corona (the sun's outer atmosphere).

Look carefully at the picture. Does it remind you of anything? Jot down any images and ideas that come to mind as you examine the black central mass of the moon and the more delicate pattern made by the sun. Perhaps the photograph will suggest ideas for a poem.

9 Bill Brandt's picture 'Portrait of a Girl, Eaton Place' on p. 29 has a strange dream-like quality about it, partly because of the unusual perspective. Look carefully at the picture and jot down any details that strike you and any images and ideas that it suggests. You may have sufficient material here for a piece of original writing.

LOVE

Sonnet 116

Let me not to the marriage of true minds
Admit impediments. Love is not love
Which alters when it alteration finds,
Or bends with the remover to remove.
O, no! it is an ever fixed mark,
That looks on tempests and is never shaken;
It is the star to every wand'ring bark,
Whose worth's unknown, although his height be taken.
Love's not Time's fool, though rosy lips and cheeks
Within his bending sickle's compass come;
Love alters not with his brief hours and weeks,
But bears it out even to the edge of doom.
    If this be error, and upon me prov'd,
    I never writ, nor no man ever lov'd.

WILLIAM SHAKESPEARE

He Wishes for the Cloths of Heaven

Had I the heavens' embroidered cloths,
Enwrought with golden and silver light,
The blue and the dim and the dark cloths
Of night and light and the half-light,
I would spread the cloths under your feet;
Tread softly because you tread on my dreams.

W. B. YEATS

Love

Two thousand cigarettes.
A hundred miles
from wall to wall.
An eternity and a half of vigils
blanker than snow.

Tons of words
old as the tracks
of a platypus in the sand.

A hundred books we didn't write.
A hundred pyramids we didn't build.

Sweepings.
Dust.

Bitter
as the beginning of the world.

Believe me when I say
it was beautiful.

MIROSLAV HOLUB
(trans. I. Milner and G. Theiner)

Plucking the Rushes

Garden rushes with red shoots,
Long leaves bending to the wind –
You and I in the same boat
Plucking rushes at the Five Lakes.
We started at dawn from the orchid-island;
We rested under the elms till noon.
You and I plucking rushes
Had not plucked a handful when night came!

ANON *(trans. Arthur Waley)*

The Picnic

It is the picnic with Ruth in the spring.
Ruth was the third on my list of seven girls
But the first two were gone (Betty) or else
Had someone (Ellen had accepted Doug).
Indian Gully the last day of school;
Girls make the lunches for the boys too.
I wrote a note to Ruth in algebra class
Day before the test. She smiled, and nodded.
We left the cars and walked through the young corn
The shoots green as paint and the leaves like tongues
Trembling. Beyond the fence where we stood
Some wild strawberry flowered by an elm tree
And Jack-in-the-pulpit was olive ripe.
A blackbird fled as I crossed, and showed
A spot of gold or red under its quick wing.
I held the wire for Ruth and watched the whip
Of her long, striped skirt as she followed.
Three freckles blossomed on her thin, white back
Underneath the loop where the blouse buttoned.
We went for our lunch away from the rest,
Stretched in the new grass, our heads close
Over unknown things wrapped up in wax papers.
Ruth tried for the same, I forget what it was,
And our hands were together. She laughed,
And a breeze caught the edge of her brown, loose hair
That touched my cheek. I turned my face into
The gentle fall. I saw how sweet it smelled.
She didn't move her head or take her hand.
I felt a soft caving in my stomach
As at the top of the highest slide
When I had been a child, but was not afraid,
And did not know why my eyes moved with wet
As I brushed her cheek with my lips and brushed
Her lips with my own lips. She said to me
Jack, Jack, different than I had ever heard,

Because she wasn't calling me, I think,
Or telling me. She used my name to
Talk in another way I wanted to know.
She laughed again and then she took her hand;
I gave her what we both had touched – can't
Remember what it was, and we ate the lunch.
Afterwards we walked in the small, cool creek
Our shoes off, her skirt hitched, and she smiling,
My pants rolled, and then we climbed up the high
Side of Indian Gully and looked
Where we had been, our hands together again.
It was then some bright thing came in my eyes,
Starting at the back of them and flowing
Suddenly through my head and down my arms
And stomach and my bare legs that seemed not
To stop in feet, nor to feel the red earth
Of the Gully, as though we hung in a
Touch of birds. There was a word in my throat
With the feeling and I knew the first time
What it meant and I said, it's beautiful.
Yes, she said, and I felt the sound and word
In my hand join the sound and word in hers
As in one name said, or in one cupped hand.
We put back on our shoes and socks and we
Sat in the grass awhile, crosslegged, under
A blowing tree, not saying anything.
And Ruth played with shells she found in the creek,
As I watched. Her small wrist which was so sweet
To me turned by her breast and the shells dropped
Green, white, blue, easily into her lap,
Passing light through themselves. She gave the pale
Shells to me, and got up and touched her hips
With her light hands, and we walked down slowly
To play the school games with the others.

JOHN LOGAN

'Attraction', *Edvard Munch*

Twice Shy

Her scarf *à la* Bardot,
In suede flats for the walk,
She came with me one evening
For air and friendly talk.
We crossed the quiet river,
Took the embankment walk.

Traffic holding its breath,
Sky a tense diaphragm :
Dusk hung like a backcloth
That shook where a swan swam,
Tremulous as a hawk
Hanging deadly, calm.

A vacuum of need
Collapsed each hunting heart
But tremulously we held
As hawk and prey apart,
Preserved classic decorum,
Deployed our talk with art.

Our juvenilia
Had taught us both to wait,
Not to publish feeling
And regret it all too late –
Mushroom loves already
Had puffed and burst in hate.

So, chary and excited
As a thrush linked on a hawk,
We thrilled to the March twilight
With nervous childish talk :
Still waters running deep
Along the embankment walk.

SEAMUS HEANEY

Night Ride

Along the black
leather strap
of the night
deserted road

swiftly rolls
the freighted bus.
Huddled together
two lovers doze

their hands linkt
across their laps
their bodies loosely
interlockt

their heads resting
two heavy fruits
on the plaited
basket of their limbs.

Slowly the bus
slides into light.
Here are hills
detach'd from dark

the road, uncoils
a white ribbon
the lovers with
the hills unfold

wake cold
to face the fate
of those who love
despite the world.

HERBERT READ

43

Dog-Tired

If she would come to me here
    Now the sunken swaths
    Are glittering paths
To the sun, and the swallows cut clear
Into the setting sun! if she came to me here!

If she would come to me now,
Before the last-mown harebells are dead
While that vetch clump still burns red!
Before all the bats have dropped from the bough
To cool in the night; if she came to me now!

The horses are untackled, the chattering machine
Is still at last. If she would come
We could gather up the dry hay from
The hill-brow, and lie quite still, till the green
Sky ceased to quiver, and lost its active sheen.

I should like to drop
On the hay, with my head on her knee,
And lie dead still, while she
Breathed quiet above me; and the crop
Of stars grew silently.

I should like to lie still
As if I was dead; but feeling
Her hand go stealing
Over my face and my head, until
This ache was shed.

D. H. LAWRENCE

Les Sylphides

Life in a day : he took his girl to the ballet;
Being shortsighted himself could hardly see it –
 The white skirts in the grey
 Glade and the swell of the music
 Lifting the white sails.

Calyx upon calyx, canterbury bells in the breeze
The flowers on the left mirror to the flowers on the right
 And the naked arms above
 The powdered faces moving
 Like seaweed in a pool.

Now, he thought, we are floating – ageless, oarless –
Now there is no separation, from now on
 You will be wearing white
 Satin and a red sash
 Under the waltzing trees.

But the music stopped, the dancers took their curtain,
The river had come to a lock – a shuffle of programmes –
 And we cannot continue down
 Stream unless we are ready
 To enter the lock and drop.

So they were married – to be the more together –
And found they were never again so much together,
 Divided by the morning tea,
 By the evening paper,
 By children and the tradesmen's bills.

Waking at times in the night she found assurance
In his regular breathing, but wondered whether
 It was really worth it and where
 The river had flowed away
 And where were the white flowers.

LOUIS MACNEICE

45

Made in Heaven

From Heals and Harrods come her lovely bridegrooms
(One cheque alone furnished two bedrooms),

From a pantechnicon in the dog-paraded street
Under the orange plane leaves, on workmen's feet

Crunching over Autumn, the fruits of marriage brought
Craftsmen-felt wood, Swedish dressers, a court

Stool tastefully imitated and the wide bed –
(the girl who married money kept her maiden head).

As things were ticked off the Harrods list, there grew
A middle-class maze to pick your way through –

The labour-saving kitchen to match the labour-saving thing
She'd fitted before marriage (O Love, with this ring

I thee wed) – lastly the stereophonic radiogram
And her Aunt's sly letter promising a pram.

Settled in now, the Italian honeymoon over,
As the relatives said, she was living in clover.

The discontented drinking of a few weeks stopped,
She woke up one morning to her husband's alarm-clock,

Saw the shining faces of the wedding gifts from the bed,
Foresaw the cosy routine of the massive years ahead.

As she watched her husband knot his tie for the city,
She thought: I wanted to be a dancer once – it's a pity

I've done none of the things I thought I wanted to,
Found nothing more exacting than my own looks, got through

Half a dozen lovers whose faces I can't quite remember
(I can still start the Rose Adagio, one foot on the fender)

But at least I'm safe from everything but cancer –
The apotheosis of the young wife and mediocre dancer.

PETER PORTER

The Passionate Shepherd to his Love

Come live with me and be my Love,
And we will all the pleasures prove
That hills and valleys, dale and field,
And all the craggy mountains yield.

There will we sit upon the rocks
And see the shepherds feed their flocks,
By shallow rivers, to whose falls
Melodious birds sing madrigals.

There will I make thee beds of roses
And a thousand fragrant posies,
A cap of flowers and a kirtle
Embroidered all with leaves of myrtle.

A gown made of the finest wool,
Which from our pretty lambs we pull,
Fair linèd slippers for the cold,
With buckles of the purest gold.

A belt of straw and ivy buds
With coral clasps and amber studs :
And if these pleasures may thee move,
Come live with me and be my Love.

Thy silver dishes for thy meat
As precious as the gods do eat,
Shall on an ivory table be
Prepared each day for thee and me.

The shepherd swains shall dance and sing
For thy delight each May-morning:
If these delights thy mind may move,
Then live with me and be my Love.

CHRISTOPHER MARLOWE

To His Coy Mistress

Had we but World enough, and Time,
This coyness Lady were no crime.
We would sit down, and think which way
To walk, and pass our long Loves Day.
Thou by the *Indian Ganges* side
Should'st Rubies find: I by the Tide
Of *Humber* would complain. I would
Love you ten years before the Flood:
And you should if you please refuse
Till the Conversion of the *Jews*.
My vegetable Love should grow
Vaster than Empires, and more slow.
An hundred years should go to praise
Thine Eyes, and on thy Forehead Gaze.
Two hundred to adore each Breast:
But thirty thousand to the rest.
An Age at least to every part,
And the last Age should show your Heart.
For Lady you deserve this State;
Nor would I love at lower rate.

But at my back I alwaies hear
Times winged Charriot hurrying near :
And yonder all before us lye
Desarts of vast Eternity.
Thy Beauty shall no more be found,
Nor, in thy marble Vault, shall sound
My ecchoing Song: then Worms shall try
That long preserv'd Virginity :
And your quaint Honour turn to dust;
And into ashes all my Lust.
The Grave's a fine and private Place,
But none I think do there embrace.
    Now therefore, while the youthful hew
Sits on thy skin like morning dew,
And while thy willing Soul transpires
At every pore with instant Fires,
Now let us sport us while we may;
And now, like am'rous birds of prey,
Rather at once our Time devour,
Than languish in his slow-chapt pow'r.
Let us roll all our Strength, and all
Our sweetness, up into one Ball :
And tear our Pleasures with rough strife,
Thorough the Iron gates of Life.
Thus, though we cannot make our Sun
Stand still, yet we will make him run.

ANDREW MARVELL

The Sunne Rising

Busie old foole, unruly Sunne,
Why dost thou thus,
Through windowes, and through curtaines call on us?
Must to thy motions lovers seasons run?
Sawcy pedantique wretch, goe chide
Late schoole boyes and sowre prentices,
Go tell Court-huntsmen, that the King will ride,
Call countrey ants to harvest offices;
Love, all alike, no season knowes, nor clyme,
Nor houres, dayes, moneths, which are the rags of time.

Thy beames, so reverend, and strong
Why shouldst thou thinke?
I could eclipse and cloud them with a winke,
But that I would not lose her sight so long:
If her eyes have not blinded thine,
Looke, and to morrow late, tell mee,
Whether both th'India's of spice and Myne
Be where thou leftest them, or lie here with mee.
Aske for those Kings whom thou saw'st yesterday,
And thou shalt heare, All here in one bed lay.

She is all States, and all Princes, I,
Nothing else is.
Princes doe but play us; compar'd to this,
All honour's mimique; All wealth alchimie.
Thou sunne art halfe as happy as wee,
In all that the world's contracted thus;
Thine age askes ease, and since thy duties bee
To warme the world, that's done in warming us.
Shine here to us, and thou art every where;
This bed thy center is, these walls, thy spheare.

JOHN DONNE

One Flesh

Lying apart now, each in a separate bed,
　He with a book, keeping the light on late,
She like a girl dreaming of childhood,
　All men elsewhere – it is as if they wait
Some new event: the book he holds unread,
Her eyes fixed on the shadows overhead.

Tossed up like flotsam from a former passion,
　How cool they lie. They hardly ever touch,
Or if they do it is like a confession
　Of having little feeling – or too much.
Chastity faces them, a destination
For which their whole lives were a preparation.

Strangely apart and strangely close together,
　Silence between them like a thread to hold
And not wind in. And time itself's a feather
　Touching them gently. Do they know they're old,
These two who are my father and mother
Whose fire, from which I came, has now grown cold?

ELIZABETH JENNINGS

When You Are Old

When you are old and grey and full of sleep,
And nodding by the fire, take down this book,
And slowly read, and dream of the soft look
Your eyes had once, and of their shadows deep.

How many loved your moments of glad grace,
And loved your beauty with love false or true,
But one man loved the pilgrim soul in you,
And loved the sorrows of your changing face;

And bending down beside the glowing bars,
Murmur, a little sadly, how Love fled
And paced upon the mountains overhead
And hid his face amid a crowd of stars.

W. B. YEATS

Neutral Tones

We stood by a pond that winter day,
And the sun was white, as though chidden of God,
And a few leaves lay on the starving sod,
   – They had fallen from an ash, and were gray.

Your eyes on me were as eyes that rove
Over tedious riddles solved years ago;
And words played between us to and fro –
   On which lost the more by our love.

The smile on your mouth was the deadest thing
Alive enough to have strength to die;
And a grin of bitterness swept thereby
   Like an ominous bird a-wing. . . .

Since then, keen lessons that love deceives,
And wrings with wrong, have shaped to me
Your face, and the God-curst sun, and a tree,
   And a pond edged with grayish leaves.

THOMAS HARDY

The Parting

Since there's no help, come let us kiss and part –
Nay, I have done, you get no more of me;
And I am glad, yea, glad with all my heart,
That thus so cleanly I myself can free.
Shake hands for ever, cancel all our vows,
And when we meet at any time again,
Be it not seen in either of our brows
That we one jot of former love retain.
Now at the last gasp of Love's latest breath,
When, his pulse failing, Passion speechless lies,
When Faith is kneeling by his bed of death,
And Innocence is closing up his eyes,
   – Now if thou wouldst, when all have given him over,
   From death to life thou might'st him yet recover.

MICHAEL DRAYTON

Intimates

Don't you care for my love? she said bitterly.

I handed her the mirror, and said :
Please address these questions to the proper person !
Please make all requests to head-quarters !
In all matters of emotional importance
please approach the supreme authority direct ! –
So I handed her the mirror.

And she would have broken it over my head,
but she caught sight of her own reflection
and that held her spellbound for two seconds
while I fled.

D. H. LAWRENCE

53

Discussion and Writing

1 John Logan's poem *The Picnic* on p. 39 describes an occasion when, for the first time, Jack, a teenager, feels some real sympathy and affection flow between himself and a girl whom he has taken on the school picnic. Notice how the writer makes the incident believable by describing carefully *in detail* the landscape of Indian Gully, the ordinary activities of picnicking, walking in the river or playing with shells, and the special feeling of attraction and happiness which develops between two people. There may be a similar experience, real or imagined, which you could write about. You might find Munch's picture *Attraction* on p. 41 a helpful way into the subject.

2 Do you have a mental image of your ideal boy or girl friend? Does this image have any basis in fact or is it, totally, a figment of your imagination? What does this image tell you about yourself? Perhaps you could write about this.

3 Herbert Read's *Night Ride* (p. 43) may remind you of an occasion when you have noticed two people showing their affection for each other quite naturally and unselfconsciously. Perhaps the turn of a head, a particular look in someone's eyes, a kiss, the holding of hands may have struck you as beautiful as the couple's relationship does Read. Try to describe, in a poem, what you see. How do you react? Envy? Embarrassment? Nervous laughter? You may want to include your feelings in your poem.

4 Try to imagine a parting between two people who have a strong affection for each other. Perhaps they are saying goodbye to each other at a station. What are their feelings? What goes on inside their minds as the time approaches? What details do they notice of their surroundings? What are their feelings after they separate?

5 Many pop songs and poems are concerned with people's feelings when a relationship breaks up. It can be a hurtful experience. Perhaps you can imagine such an experience and write about it.

6 One situation you may have faced already and which you are almost certain to face in the future is visiting the boy or girl friend's home for the first time and meeting his or her parents. There is scope for a piece of writing here based on such a situation, either real or imagined.

WAR

Futility

Move him into the sun –
Gently its touch awoke him once,
At home, whispering of fields unsown.
Always it woke him, even in France,
Until this morning and this snow.
If anything might rouse him now
The kind old sun will know.

Think how it wakes the seeds, –
Woke, once, the clays of a cold star.
Are limbs, so dear-achieved, are sides,
Full-nerved – still warm – too hard to stir?
Was it for this the clay grew tall?
– O what made fatuous sunbeams toil
To break earth's sleep at all?

WILFRED OWEN

[A dead German outside his dug-out, Beaumont-Hamel, November 1916.
Photo: Imperial War Museum

Disabled

He sat in a wheeled chair, waiting for dark,
And shivered in his ghastly suit of grey,
Legless, sewn short at elbow. Through the park
Voices of boys rang saddening like a hymn,
Voices of play and pleasure after day,
Till gathering sleep had mothered them from him.

About this time Town used to swing so gay
When glow-lamps budded in the light blue trees,
And girls glanced lovelier as the air grew dim, –
In the old times, before he threw away his knees.
Now he will never feel again how slim
Girls' waists are, or how warm their subtle hands;
All of them touch him like some queer disease.

There was an artist silly for his face,
For it was younger than his youth, last year.
Now, he is old; his back will never brace;
He's lost his colour very far from here,
Poured it down shell-holes till the veins ran dry,
And half his lifetime lapsed in the hot race,
And leap of purple spurted from his thigh.

One time he liked a blood-smear down his leg,
After the matches, carried shoulder-high.
It was after football, when he'd drunk a peg,
He thought he'd better join. – He wonders why.
Someone had said he'd look a god in kilts,
That's why; and may be, too, to please his Meg;
Aye, that was it, to please the giddy jilts
He asked to join. He didn't have to beg;
Smiling they wrote his lie; aged nineteen years.
Germans he scarcely thought of; all their guilt,

And Austria's, did not move him. And no fears
Of Fear came yet. He thought of jewelled hilts
For daggers in plaid socks; of smart salutes;
And care of arms; and leave; and pay arrears;
Esprit de corps; and hints for young recruits.
And soon, he was drafted out with drums and cheers.

Some cheered him home, but not as crowds cheer Goal.
Only a solemn man who brought him fruits
Thanked him; and then inquired about his soul.

Now, he will spend a few sick years in Institutes,
And do what things the rules consider wise,
And take whatever pity they may dole.
To-night he noticed how the women's eyes
Passed from him to the strong men that were whole.
How cold and late it is! Why don't they come
And put him into bed? Why don't they come?

WILFRED OWEN

First World War Recruiting Poster, *Imperial War Museum*

'Blighters'

The House is crammed : tier beyond tier they grin
And cackle at the Show, while prancing ranks
Of harlots shrill the chorus, drunk with din;
'We're sure the Kaiser loves our dear old Tanks!'

I'd like to see a Tank come down the stalls,
Lurching to rag-time tunes, or 'Home, sweet Home',
And there'd be no more jokes in Music-halls
To mock the riddled corpses round Bapaume.

SIEGFRIED SASSOON

First World War Recruiting Poster, *Imperial War Museum*

The General

'Good-morning; good-morning!' the General said
When we met him last week on our way to the line.
Now the soldiers he smiled at are most of 'em dead,
And we're cursing his staff for incompetent swine.
'He's a cheery old card,' grunted Harry to Jack
As they slogged up to Arras with rifle and pack.

   .   .   .   .

But he did for them both by his plan of attack.

SIEGFRIED SASSOON

Lamentations

I found him in the guard-room at the Base.
From the blind darkness I had heard his crying
And blundered in. With puzzled, patient face
A sergeant watched him; it was no good trying
To stop it; for he howled and beat his chest.
And, all because his brother had gone west,
Raved at the bleeding war; his rampant grief
Moaned, shouted, sobbed, and choked, while he was kneeling
Half-naked on the floor. In my belief
Such men have lost all patriotic feeling.

SIEGFRIED SASSOON

Naming of Parts

Today we have naming of parts. Yesterday,
We had daily cleaning. And tomorrow morning
We shall have what to do after firing. But today,
Today we have naming of parts. Japonica
Glistens like coral in all of the neighbouring gardens,
    And to-day we have naming of parts.

This is the lower sling swivel. And this
Is the upper sling swivel, whose use you will see,
When you are given your slings. And this is the piling swivel,
Which in your case you have not got. The branches
Hold in the gardens their silent, eloquent gestures,
    Which in our case we have not got.

This is the safety-catch, which is always released
With an easy flick of the thumb. And please do not let me
See anyone using his finger. You can do it quite easy
If you have any strength in your thumb. The blossoms
Are fragile and motionless, never letting anyone see
    Any of them using their finger.

And this you can see is the bolt. The purpose of this
Is to open the breech, as you see. We can slide it
Rapidly backwards and forwards: we call this
Easing the spring. And rapidly backwards and forwards
The early bees are assaulting and fumbling the flowers;
    They call it easing the Spring.

They call it easing the Spring: it is perfectly easy
If you have any strength in your thumb: like the bolt,
And the breech, and the cocking-piece, and the point of balance,
Which in our case we have not got; and the almond-blossom
Silent in all of the gardens and the bees going backwards and
  forwards,
    For today we have naming of parts.

HENRY REED

Bayonet Charge

Suddenly he awoke and was running – raw
In raw-seamed hot khaki, his sweat heavy,
Stumbling across a field of clods towards a green hedge
That dazzled with rifle fire, hearing
Bullets smacking the belly out of the air –
He lugged a rifle numb as a smashed arm;
The patriotic tear that had brimmed in his eye
Sweating like molten iron from the centre of his chest, –

In bewilderment then he almost stopped –
In what cold clockwork of the stars and the nations
Was he the hand pointing that second? He was running
Like a man who has jumped up in the dark and runs
Listening between his footfalls for the reason
Of his still running, and his foot hung like
Statuary in mid-stride. Then the shot-slashed furrows

Threw up a yellow hare that rolled like a flame
And crawled in a threshing circle, its mouth wide
Open silent, its eyes standing out.
He plunged past with his bayonet toward the green hedge.
King, honour, human dignity, etcetera
Dropped like luxuries in a yelling alarm
To get out of that blue crackling air
His terror's touchy dynamite.

TED HUGHES

Landscape with Figures

I

Perched on a great fall of air
a pilot or angel looking down
on some eccentric chart, a plain
dotted with useless furniture,
discerns dying on the sand vehicles
squashed dead or still entire, stunned
like beetles : scattered wingcases and
legs, heads, appear when the dust settles.
But you who like Thomas come
to poke fingers in the wounds
find monuments and metal posies.
On each disordered tomb
the steel is torn into fronds
by the lunatic explosive.

II

On sand and scrub the dead men wriggle
in their dowdy clothes. They are mimes
who express silence and futile aims
enacting this prone and motionless struggle
at a queer angle to the scenery,
crawling on the boards of the stage like walls,
deaf to the one who opens his mouth and calls
silently. The decor is a horrible tracery
of iron. The eye and mouth of each figure
bear the cosmetic blood and the hectic
colours death has the only list of.
A yard more and my little finger
could trace the maquillage of these stony actors :
I am the figure writhing on the backcloth.

KEITH DOUGLAS

No More Hiroshimas

At the station exit, my bundle in hand,
Early the winter afternoon's wet snow
Falls thinly round me, out of a crudded sun.
I had forgotten to remember where I was.
Looking about, I see it might be anywhere –
A station, a town like any other in Japan,
Ramshackle, muddy, noisy, drab; a cheerfully
Shallow permanence : peeling concrete, litter, 'Atomic
Lotion, for hair fall-out,' a flimsy department-store;
Racks and towers of neon, flashy over tiled and tilted waves
Of little roofs, shacks cascading lemons and persimmons,
Oranges and dark-red apples, shanties awash with rainbows
Of squid and octopus, shellfish, slabs of tuna, oysters, ice,
Ablaze with fans of soiled nude-picture books
Thumbed abstractedly by schoolboys, with second-hand looks.

The river remains unchanged, sad, refusing rehabilitation.
In this long, wide, empty official boulevard
The new trees are still small, the office blocks
Basely functional, the bridge a slick abstraction.
But the river remains unchanged, sad, refusing rehabilitation.

In the city centre, far from the station's lively squalor,
A kind of life goes on, in cinemas and hi-fi coffee bars,
In the shuffling racket of pin-table palaces and parlours,
The souvenir-shops piled with junk, kimonoed kewpie-dolls,
Models of the bombed Industry Promotion Hall, memorial ruin
Tricked out with glitter-frost and artificial pearls.

Set in an awful emptiness, the modern tourist hotel is trimmed
With jaded Christmas frippery, flatulent balloons; in the hall,
A giant dingy iced cake in the shape of a Cinderella coach.
The contemporary stairs are treacherous, the corridors
Deserted, my room an overheated morgue, the bar in darkness.
Punctually, the electric chimes ring out across the tidy waste
Their doleful public hymn – the tune unrecognizable, evangelist.

Here atomic peace is geared to meet the tourist trade.
Let it remain like this, for all the world to see,
Without nobility or loveliness, and dogged with shame
That is beyond all hope of indignation. Anger, too, is dead.
And why should memorials of what was far
From pleasant have the grace that helps us to forget?

In the dying afternoon, I wander dying round the Park of Peace.
It is right, this squat, dead place, with its left-over air
Of an abandoned International Trade and Tourist Fair.
The stunted trees are wrapped in straw against the cold.
The gardeners are old, old women in blue bloomers, white
     aprons,
Survivors weeding the dead brown lawns around the Children's
Monument.

A hideous pile, the Atomic Bomb Explosion Centre, freezing
     cold,
'Includes the Peace Tower, a museum containing
Atomic-melted slates and bricks, photos showing
What the Atomic Desert looked like, and other
Relics of the catastrophe.'

The other relics:
The ones that made me weep;
The bits of burnt clothing,
The stopped watches, the torn shirts.
The twisted buttons,
The stained and tattered vests and drawers,
The ripped kimonos and charred boots,
The white blouse polka-dotted with atomic rain, indelible,
The cotton summer pants the blasted boys crawled home in,
     to bleed
And slowly die.

Remember only these.
They are the memorials we need.

                                        JAMES KIRKUP

Relative Sadness

Einstein's eyes
were filled with tears
when he heard about Hiroshima.
Mr. Tamihi
had no eyes left
to show his grief.

COLIN ROWBOTHAM

Fall 1961

Back and forth, back and forth
goes the tock, tock, tock
of the orange, bland, ambassadorial
face of the moon
on the grandfather clock.

All autumn, the chafe and jar
of nuclear war;
we have talked our extinction to death.
I swim like a minnow
behind my studio window.

Our end drifts nearer,
the moon lifts,
radiant with terror.
The state
is a diver under a glass bell.

A father's no shield
for his child.
We are like a lot of wild
spiders crying together,
but without tears.

Nature holds up a mirror.
One swallow makes a summer.
It's easy to tick
off the minutes,
but the clockhands stick.

Back and forth!
Back and forth, back and forth –
my one point of rest
is the orange and black
oriole's swinging nest!

ROBERT LOWELL

Your Attention Please

YOUR ATTENTION PLEASE –
The Polar DEW has just warned that
A nuclear rocket strike of
At least one thousand megatons
Has been launched by the enemy
Directly at our major cities.
This announcement will take
Two and a quarter minutes to make,
You therefore have a further
Eight and a quarter minutes
To comply with the shelter
Requirements published in the Civil
Defence Code – section Atomic Attack.
A specially shortened Mass
Will be broadcast at the end
Of this announcement –
Protestant and Jewish services
Will begin simultaneously –
Select your wavelength immediately
According to instructions
In the Defence Code. Do not
Take well-loved pets (including birds)
Into your shelter – they will consume
Fresh air. Leave the old and bed-
Ridden, you can do nothing for them.
Remember to press the sealing
Switch when everyone is in
The shelter. Set the radiation
Aerial, turn on the geiger barometer.
Turn off your Television now.
Turn off your radio immediately
The services end. At the same time
Secure explosion plugs in the ears
Of each member of your family. Take
Down your plasma flasks. Give your children

The pills marked one and two
In the C.D. green container, then put
Them to bed. Do not break
The inside airlock seals until
The radiation All Clear shows
(Watch for the cuckoo in your
Perspex panel), or your District
Touring Doctor rings your bell.
If before this your air becomes
Exhausted or if any of your family
Is critically injured, administer
The capsules marked 'Valley Forge'
(Red pocket in No. 1 Survival Kit)
For painless death. (Catholics
Will have been instructed by their priests
What to do in this eventuality.)
This announcement is ending. Our President
Has already given orders for
Massive retaliation – it will be
Decisive. Some of us may die.
Remember, statistically
It is not likely to be you.
All flags are flying fully dressed
On Government buildings – the sun is shining.
Death is the least we have to fear.
We are all in the hands of God,
Whatever happens happens by His will.
Now go quickly to your shelters.

PETER PORTER

The Forest

Among the primary rocks
where the bird spirits
crack the granite seeds
and the tree statues
with their black arms
threaten the clouds,

suddenly
there comes a rumble,
as if history
were being uprooted,

the grass bristles,
boulders tremble,
the earth's surface cracks

and there grows

a mushroom,

immense as life itself,
filled with billions of cells
immense as life itself,
eternal,
watery,

appearing in this world for the first

and last time.

MIROSLAV HOLUB

(*trans. I. Milner and G. Theiner*)

'Atom Piece', *Henry Moore*

The Horses

Barely a twelvemonth after
The seven days war that put the world to sleep,
Late in the evening the strange horses came.
By then we had made our covenant with silence,
But in the first few days it was so still
We listened to our breathing and were afraid.
On the second day
The radios failed; we turned the knobs; no answer.
On the third day a warship passed us, heading north,
Dead bodies piled on the deck. On the sixth day
A plane plunged over us into the sea. Thereafter
Nothing. The radios dumb;
And still they stand in corners of our kitchens,
And stand, perhaps, turned on, in a million rooms
All over the world. But now if they should speak,
If on a sudden they should speak again,
If on the stroke of noon a voice should speak,
We would not listen, we would not let it bring
That bad old world that swallowed its children quick
At one great gulp. We would not have it again.
Sometimes we think of the nations lying asleep,
Curled blindly in impenetrable sorrow,
And then the thought confounds us with its strangeness.

The tractors lie about our fields; at evening
They look like dank sea-monsters crouched and waiting.
We leave them where they are and let them rust :
"They'll moulder away and be like other loam."
We make our oxen drag our rusty ploughs,
Long laid aside. We have gone back
Far past our fathers' land.
                              And then, that evening
Late in the summer the strange horses came.
We heard a distant tapping on the road,
A deepening drumming; it stopped, went on again,
And at the corner changed to hollow thunder.

74

We saw the heads
Like a wild wave charging and were afraid.
We had sold our horses in our fathers' time
To buy new tractors. Now they were strange to us
As fabulous steeds set on an ancient shield
Or illu   ns in a book of knights.
We d   are go near them. Yet they waited,
          d shy, as if they had been sent
          ommand to find our whereabouts
          ng-lost archaic companionship.
          moment we had never a thought
          were creatures to be owned and used.
          m were some half-a-dozen colts
          n some wilderness of the broken world,
          s if they had come from their own Eden.
          n they have pulled our ploughs and borne our loads,
          free servitude still can pierce our hearts.
          s changed; their coming our beginning.

EDWIN MUIR

Ordinary Sunday

        inary Sunday. First the light
        g dead through dormitory windows blind
        og; and then, at breakfast, every plate
        d with the small, red cotton flower; and no
        nce for pocketmoney. Greatcoats, lined
By the right, marched from their pegs, with slow
Poppy fires smouldering in one lapel
To light us through the fallen cloud. Behind
That handkerchief sobbed the quick Sunday bell.

A granite cross, the school field underfoot,
Inaudible prayers, hymn-sheets that stirred
Too loudly in the hand. When hymns ran out,
Silence, like silt, lay round so wide and deep
It seemed that winter held its breath. We heard
Only the river talking in its sleep:
Until the bugler flexed his lips, and sound
Cutting the fog cleanly like a bird,
Circled and sang out over the bandaged ground.

Then, low voiced, the headmaster called the roll
Of those who could not answer; every name
Suffixed with honour – 'double first', 'kept goal
For Cambridge' – and a death – in spitfires, tanks,
And ships torpedoed. At his call there came
Through the mist blond heroes in broad ranks
With rainbows struggling on their chests. Ahead
Of us, in strict step, as we idled home
Marched the formations of the towering dead.

November again, and the bugles blown
In a tropical Holy Trinity,
The heroes today stand further off, grown
Smaller but distinct. They flash no medals, keep
No ranks: through *Last Post* and *Reveille*
Their chins loll on their chests, like birds asleep.
Only when the long, last note ascends
Upon the wings of kites, some two or three
Look up: and have the faces of my friends.

                                        JON STALLWORTHY

THE COST

In World War 1 armed forces on both sides totalled 65 million. Of these 8,538,000 were killed and 21,205,000 wounded.

THE ALLIES

5,152,000 dead
12,817,000 wounded

THE ENEMY

3,386,000 dead
8,388,000 wounded

MANPOWER

ALLIES:

Russia	Strength 12 million
	Killed 1,700,000
British	Strength 9 million
Empire	Killed 908,000
France	Strength $8\frac{1}{2}$ million
	Killed 1,358,000
Italy	Strength $5\frac{1}{2}$ million
	Killed 650,000
USA	Strength 4 million
	Killed 126,000

CENTRAL POWERS:

Germany	Strength 11 million
	Killed 1,773,000
Austro-	Strength 8 million
Hungary	Killed 1,200,000
Turkey	Strength 3 million
	Killed 325,000

CASUALTIES

Numerically, Russia, Germany, the Austro-Hungarian Empire and France were the biggest sufferers in men killed, wounded, missing or taken prisoner. But the loss to the British Empire was comparatively just as heavy:
12 per cent of the adult male population of Britain
10 per cent of the adult male population of New Zealand
9 per cent of the adult male population of Australia
6 per cent of the adult male population of Canada
were casualties.

LIFE EXPECTATION

Life expectation for officers at the front was about 5 months in 1914; about 10 months in 1918
For every officer killed 20 men were killed
Average British casualties a month:

	Officers	All Ranks
1914	900	18,450
1915	925	19,000
1916	2154	44,000
1917	2766	56,800
1918	3680	75,500

At the Battle of the Somme on July 1, 1916, the British lost 15 men killed and 25 men wounded a minute for 24 hours

PRISONERS

The ALLIES took 3,600,000 – $2\frac{1}{4}$ million Austro-Hungarians and over 1 million Germans

The ENEMY took 4 million –
$2\frac{1}{2}$ million from Russia
$\frac{1}{2}$ million from Italy
$\frac{1}{2}$ million from France
and fewer than 200,000
from the British Empire

Discussion and Writing

In the corresponding section of Book Three we suggested some of the dangers and advantages of trying to write war poems from your own second-hand experience of war. Whether or not you recall this section, it will be helpful to discuss amongst yourselves why you imagine we think this subject may present dangers and difficulties and why, on balance, we decided that this is a worthwhile and valuable experience.

In Book Three we concentrated mainly on poems which described the people and incidents in war, many of them from the 1914–1918 period. In Book Four there were more poems from the 1939–1945 period, several of which raised specific issues about the rights and wrongs of warfare. Here, poems from both world wars are represented, together with a number of pieces which describe nuclear warfare.

1 On page 77 we have printed some statistics about the First World War. After you have read these through and, perhaps, discussed them amongst yourselves, turn to the group of poems on pages 55 to 64. The poems and the horrifying picture on p. 56 will help to make these cold facts more real and meaningful and the contrast between a page of statistics and a soldier's poem may suggest an idea to you for a piece of writing.

2 Henry Moore's sculpture, *Atom Piece* (p. 73), contains a number of metaphors. What can you *see* in the shape? A mushroom cloud? a skull? a bomb-shell? What is the effect of the scratched surfaces in the lower part of the sculpture below the contrasting smoothness of the dome? Perhaps you could write your own *Atom Piece* in words: maybe one in which you put down what is suggested to you by this sculpture, or a poem in which you protest against these images of horror.

3 In *No Ordinary Sunday* on p. 75, Jon Stallworthy recounts his memory of Remembrance Sunday from his schooldays. When you have looked at this poem you may want to talk about the whole purpose of remembrance. By its nature it is retrospective and runs the danger of being merely nostalgic.

Should Remembrance Day be forward-looking as well as backward-looking?

Should November 11th be a more positive occasion when we not only *remember* suffering but when we try also to *relieve* it by linking this day with, say, a National Oxfam Day?

Should we remember the German dead as well as the English?

Your discussion may suggest a piece of writing to you. The special seriousness and atmosphere of the remembrance service, the poppy symbol, the sight of old soldiers around a war memorial – there are several possibilities here for a poem.

4 The poems on pp. 66 to 75 evoke, in different ways, the frightful consequences of push-button warfare and imply the insanity and unreality of a horror with which the mind can scarcely come to terms. Perhaps these poems, television documentaries or a film like *The War Game* which you may have seen, will suggest a piece of writing about a possible Third World War to you.

5 Both the posters from the First World War recruiting campaign are attempts by the government to put emotional and moral pressure on the men of Britain to enlist. Discuss the message of each poster and the ways in which they work. In the light of what we know of the Great War, now that it is long over, does the appeal seem justified? Look at some of Owen's and Sassoon's poems to help you put the pictures in perspective.

Perhaps you could find the basis for an original piece of writing either in these posters or in a modern recruiting poster for one of the armed forces.

RELIGIOUS EXPERIENCE

Church Going

Once I am sure there's nothing going on
I step inside, letting the door thud shut.
Another church: matting, seats, and stone,
And little books; sprawlings of flowers, cut
For Sunday, brownish now; some brass and stuff
Up at the holy end; the small neat organ;
And a tense, musty, unignorable silence,
Brewed God knows how long. Hatless, I take off
My cycle-clips in awkward reverence,

Move forward, run my hand around the font.
From where I stand, the roof looks almost new –
Cleaned, or restored? Someone would know: I don't.
Mounting the lectern, I peruse a few
Hectoring large-scale verses, and pronounce
"Here endeth" much more loudly than I'd meant.
The echoes snigger briefly. Back at the door
I sign the book, donate an Irish sixpence,
Reflect the place was not worth stopping for.

Yet stop I did: in fact I often do,
And always end much at a loss like this,
Wondering what to look for; wondering, too,
When churches fall completely out of use
What we shall turn them into, if we shall keep
A few cathedrals chronically on show,
Their parchment, plate and pyx in locked cases,
And let the rest rent free to rain and sheep.
Shall we avoid them as unlucky places?

Or, after dark, will dubious women come
To make their children touch a particular stone;
Pick simples for a cancer; or on some
Advised night see walking a dead one?
Power of some sort or other will go on
In games, in riddles, seemingly at random;
But superstition, like belief, must die,
And what remains when disbelief has gone?
Grass, weedy pavements, brambles, buttress, sky,

A shape less recognisable each week,
A purpose more obscure. I wonder who
Will be the last, the very last, to seek
This place for what it was; one of the crew
That tap and jot and know what rood-lofts were?
Some ruin-bibber, randy for antique,
Or Christmas-addict, counting on a whiff
Of gown-and-bands and organ-pipes and myrrh?
Or will he be my representative,

Bored, uninformed, knowing the ghostly silt
Dispersed, yet tending to this cross of ground
Through suburb scrub because it held unspilt
So long and equably what since is found
Only in separation – marriage, and birth,
And death, and thoughts of these – for whom was built
This special shell? For, though I've no idea
What this accoutred frowsty barn is worth,
It pleases me to stand in silence here;

A serious house on serious earth it is,
In whose blent air all our compulsions meet,
Are recognised, and robed as destinies.
And that much never can be obsolete,
Since someone will forever be surprising
A hunger in himself to be more serious,
And gravitating with it to this ground,
Which, he once heard, was proper to grow wise in,
If only that so many dead lie round.

PHILIP LARKIN

Three Priests. *Photo: Henri Cartier-Bresson*

What Are They Thinking . . .

What are they thinking, the people in churches,
Closing their eyelids and kneeling to pray,
Touching their faces and sniffing their fingers,
Folding their knuckles one over another?
What are they thinking? Do they remember
This is the church: and this is the steeple:
Open the door: and here are the people?
Do they still see the parson climbing upstairs,
Opening the window and saying his prayers?
Do they perceive in the pit of their palms
The way of the walls and the spin of the spire,
The turmoil of tombstones tossed in the grass,
Under the yawning billows of yew?
Can they discover, drooping beyond them,
The chestnuts' fountains of flowers and frills,
And the huge fields folded into the hills?

What are they thinking, the sheep on the hills,
Bobbing and bending to nibble the grass,
Kissing the crisp green coat of the combes?
What are they thinking, lying contented
With vacant regard in long rumination?
Do they consider the sky as a cage,
Their fleeces as fetters, their bones as their bonds?
Or do they rejoice at the thyme on their tongues,
The dome of the sky, the slope of the downs,
The village below, the church, and the steeple,
With shepherd and ploughman and parson and people?

And what is he feeling, the lark as he flies,
Does he consider the span of his days,
Does he dissever himself from his spirit,
His flight from his feathers, his song from his singing?
Is he cast down at the thought of his brevity?
Or does he look forward to long immortality?

He stitches the sky with the thread of his breath
To all the bright pattern of living beneath,
To ploughman and shepherd and parson and people,
To the sheep on the hills and the church and the steeple.

BRYAN GUINNESS

The Collar

I struck the board, and cry'd, No more.
                    I will abroad.
        What? shall I ever sigh and pine?
My lines and life are free; free as the rode,
            Loose as the winde, as large as store.
            Shall I be still in suit?
        Have I no harvest but a thorn
        To let me bloud, and not restore
        What I have lost with cordiall fruit?
                    Sure there was wine
Before my sighs did drie it: there was corn
            Before my tears did drown it.
        Is the yeare onely lost to me?
            Have I no bayes to crown it?
No flowers, no garlands gay? all blasted?
            All wasted?
        Not so, my heart: but there is fruit,
                    And thou hast hands.
        Recover all thy sigh-blown age
On double pleasures: leave thy cold dispute
Of what is fit, and not. Forsake thy cage,
                    Thy rope of sands,
Which pettie thoughts have made, and made to thee
        Good cable, to enforce and draw,
                    And be thy law,
            While thou didst wink and wouldst not see,
                    Away; take heed:
                    I will abroad.

Call in thy deaths head there : tie up thy fears.
                    He that forbears
              To suit and serve his need,
                    Deserves his load.
But as I rav'd and grew more fierce and wilde
                    At every word,
        Me thoughts I heard one calling, *Child!*
              And I reply'd, *My Lord*.

The Windows

Lord, how can man preach thy eternall word?
    He is a brittle crazie glasse :
Yet in thy temple thou dost him afford
    This glorious and transcendent place,
    To be a window, through thy grace.

But when thou dost anneal in glasse thy storie,
    Making thy life to shine within
The holy Preachers; then the light and glorie
    More rev'rend grows, and more doth win;
    Which else shows watrish, bleak, and thin.

Doctrine and life, colours and light, in one
    When they combine and mingle, bring
A strong regard and aw : but speech alone
    Doth vanish like a flaring thing,
    And in the eare, not conscience ring.

God's Grandeur

The world is charged with the grandeur of God.
   It will flame out, like shining from shook foil;
   It gathers to a greatness, like the ooze of oil
Crushed. Why do men then now not reck his rod?
Generations have trod, have trod, have trod;
   And all is seared with trade; bleared, smeared with toil;
   And wears man's smudge and shares man's smell : the soil
Is bare now, nor can foot feel, being shod.

And for all this, nature is never spent;
   There lives the dearest freshness deep down things;
And though the last lights off the black West went
   Oh, morning, at the brown brink eastward, springs –
Because the Holy Ghost over the bent
   World broods with warm breast and with ah! bright wings.

GERARD MANLEY HOPKINS

A Hymne to God the Father

Wilt thou forgive that sinne where I begunne,
   Which is my sin, though it were done before?
Wilt thou forgive those sinnes through which I runne,
   And do run still : though still I do deplore?
   When thou hast done, thou hast not done,
         For, I have more.

Wilt thou forgive that sinne by which I wonne
   Others to sinne? and, made my sinne their doore?
Wilt thou forgive that sinne which I did shunne
   A yeare, or two : but wallowed in, a score?
   When thou hast done, thou hast not done,
         For, I have more.

I have a sinne of feare, that when I have spunne
    My last thred, I shall perish on the shore;
Sweare by thy selfe, that at my death thy Sunne
    Shall shine as it shines now, and heretofore;
    And, having done that, Thou hast done,
            I feare no more.

JOHN DONNE

Advent

Ice-floes lie along the river,
like disused
wrappings
of life.

The church on the common is falling apart,
the vestry is leaking,
the altar candles are snuffling.

The Lord Himself has got the shivers.

He creeps
into the hen-house across the way
and sits nodding on the roost.

He lays no eggs,
nor does he crow.

Ice-floes lie along the river
like disused
wrapppings
of life.

MIROSLAV HOLUB
(trans. I. Milner and G. Theiner)

Jigsaws V

Although we say we disbelieve,
God comes in handy when we swear –
It may be when we exult or grieve,
It may be just to clear the air;
Let the skew runner breast the tape,
Let the great lion leave his lair,
Let the hot nymph solicit rape,
We need a God to phrase it fair;
When death curls over in the wave
Strings may soar and brass may blare
But, to be frightened or be brave,
We crave some emblem for despair,
And when ice burns and joys are pain
And shadows grasp us by the hair
We need one Name to take in vain,
One taboo to break, one sin to dare.
What is it then we disbelieve?
Because the facts are far from bare
And all religions must deceive
And every proof must wear and tear,
That God exists we cannot show,
So do not know but need not care.
Thank God we do not know; we know
We need the unknown. The Unknown is There.

LOUIS MACNEICE

The Killing

That was the day they killed the Son of God
On a squat hill-top by Jerusalem.
Zion was bare, her children from their maze
Sucked by the demon curiosity
Clean through the gates. The very halt and blind
Had somehow got themselves up to the hill.

After the ceremonial preparation,
The scourging, nailing, nailing against the wood,
Erection of the main-trees with their burden,
While from the hill rose an orchestral wailing,
They were there at last, high up in the soft spring day.
We watched the writhings, heard the moanings, saw
The three heads turning on their separate axles
Like broken wheels left spinning. Round *his* head
Was loosely bound a crown of plaited thorn
That hurt at random, stinging temple and brow
As the pain swung into its envious circle.
In front the wreath was gathered in a knot
That as he gazed looked like the last stump left
Of a death-wounded deer's great antlers. Some
Who came to stare grew silent as they looked,
Indignant or sorry. But the hardened old
And the hard-hearted young, although at odds
From the first morning, cursed him with one curse,
Having prayed for a Rabbi or an armed Messiah
And found the Son of God. What use to them
Was a God or a Son of God? Of what avail
For purposes such as theirs? Beside the cross-foot,
Alone, four women stood and did not move
All day. The sun revolved, the shadow wheeled,
The evening fell. His head lay on his breast,
But in his breast they watched his heart move on
By itself alone, accomplishing its journey.

Their taunts grew louder, sharpened by the knowledge
That he was walking in the park of death,
Far from their rage. Yet all grew stale at last,
Spite, curiosity, envy, hate itself.
They waited only for death and death was slow
And came so quietly they scarce could mark it.
They were angry then with death and death's deceit.

I was a stranger, could not read these people
Or this outlandish deity. Did a God
Indeed in dying cross my life that day
By chance, he on his road and I on mine?

EDWIN MUIR

Seven Stanzas at Easter

Make no mistake: if He rose at all
it was as His body;
if the cells' dissolution did not reverse, the molecules
    reknit, the amino acids rekindle,
the Church will fall.

It was not as the flowers,
each soft Spring recurrent;
it was not as His Spirit in the mouths and fuddled
    eyes of the eleven apostles;
it was as His flesh: ours.

The same hinged thumbs and toes,
the same valved heart
that – pierced – died, withered, paused, and then
    regathered out of enduring Might
new strength to enclose.

Let us not mock God with metaphor,
analogy, sidestepping, transcendence;
making of the event a parable, a sign painted in the
      faded credulity of earlier ages :
let us walk through the door.

The stone is rolled back, not papier-mâché,
not a stone in a story,
but the vast rock of materiality that in the slow
      grinding of time will eclipse for each of us
the wide light of day.

And if we will have an angel at the tomb,
make it a real angel,
weighty with Max Planck's quanta, vivid with hair,
      opaque in the dawn light, robed in real linen
spun on a definite loom.

Let us not seek to make it less monstrous,
for our own convenience, our own sense of beauty,
lest, awakened in one unthinkable hour, we are
      embarrassed by the miracle,
      and crushed by remonstrance.

JOHN UPDIKE

Sometime During Eternity

Sometime during eternity
some guys show up
and one of them
who shows up real late
is a kind of carpenter
from some square-type place
like Galilee
and he starts wailing
and claiming he is hip
to who made heaven
and earth
and that the cat
who really laid it on us
is his Dad
And moreover
he adds
It's all writ down
on some scroll-type parchments
which some henchmen
leave lying around the Dead Sea somewheres
a long time ago
and which you won't even find
for a coupla thousand years or so
or at least for
nineteen hundred and fortyseven
of them
to be exact
and even then
nobody really believes them
or me
for that matter

You're hot
they tell him
And they cool him
They stretch him on the Tree to cool
        And everybody after that
                        is always making models
            of this Tree
                    with Him hung up
and always crooning his name
                        and calling Him to come down
            and sit in
                    on their combo
        as if he is *the* king cat
                    who's got to blow
    or they can't quite make it
Only he don't come down
                    from His Tree
Him just hang there
            on His Tree
                    looking real Petered out
            and real cool
                    and also
    according to a roundup
                of late world news
from the usual unreliable sources
                    real dead.
                    LAWRENCE FERLINGHETTI

93

Discussion and Writing

The poems in this section show many different attitudes towards religious experience. Some of you may have felt drawn to the agnosticism of Philip Larkin's *Church Going* (p. 80), others to the questioning, restless Christianity of Herbert's *The Collar* (p. 84), others again to the exulting praise and worship of Hopkins' *God's Grandeur* (p. 86). Before you attempt any writing it is worth discussing these two questions.

Do you feel that you must share the religious attitude or belief expressed in a poem in order to be able to *enjoy* that poem?

If you find yourself out of sympathy with what a poem says, does this prevent you from *appreciating* the poem as a piece of writing?

It may help to use the three poems mentioned above as evidence to support your views.

1 What, if any, is your image of God?

A force behind the cosmos which you sense, perhaps, when you look at the night sky?

The creative power which you are aware of in the beauty and design of nature?

An old man with a long white beard, like a dignified Father Christmas, who lives somewhere 'up there'?

A mental image of your 'better self' (perhaps you call it your conscience) which offers you a measure of psychological security?

However you see God, as power or beauty, a person or an illusion, it will help you to understand and clarify your ideas if you try to write about them.

2 Whether or not you are a religious person, most of you will know the outlines of the Genesis story in which the beginning of the world is portrayed as a six-day labour involving the creation of heaven and earth, light and darkness, land and sea, the stars and planets, plants and creatures and finally, man and woman in the legendary characters of Adam and Eve. It is worth reading the first chapter of Genesis to remind yourself of these images of creation.

How do *you* imagine it all began? Perhaps you could write a poem about the beginnings of the universe, suggested either by Genesis or by modern science.

3 Man, like God in the Genesis story, rests on the seventh day. Suburban Sundays are quite unlike any other days in the week.

How do you notice the difference? Jot down as many details as you can about people's behaviour, moods, pastimes or chores on a typical Sunday. You may be able to write a poem which captures the particular atmosphere of Sunday by working on some of these ideas.

4 On pp. 89–93 we have printed a group of poems about Easter, the main festival of the Christian calendar which focuses our attention upon a young man who claimed to be God and who was murdered by those who disbelieved him. The poems – all different in their attitude to Easter – may set you thinking about the death of Christ and what it means to you. Try to write about it.

5 Bryan Guinness's poem on p. 83 asks the question 'What are they thinking these people in churches?' and as you look around at the congregation in any place of worship the same question is almost bound to cross your mind. What *are* they thinking as they pray, as they listen to the sermon, as they sing? Perhaps you could write a poem which answers the question by trying to enter the minds of various members of the congregation – old ladies, teenagers, small children, housewives, and so on.

6 It is worth asking yourself not only what the people are thinking but also what goes on in the mind of the central figure in a religious service – the priest, the vicar, the minister. The photograph on p. 82 shows three Italian priests at midnight mass. Look carefully at the picture and at the faces of the three men. How do they appear to you? What are *they* thinking? You may have the basis for a piece of original writing here.

7 If you sometimes take part in religious ceremonies or services – perhaps as a server or a reader – you might be able to write about your attitude towards what you are doing and explain what you feel.

8 Many writers have felt when faced with even the simplest things – a flower, a grain of sand, a bird's nest – that if they could fully understand the miracle that made them they would understand the central mysteries of life and the universe. Do any things that we take for granted seem to you like everyday miracles? Perhaps you could discuss this and use your ideas as the basis for a poem.

[Confrontation: Pentagon, Washington. *Photo: Marc Riboud*

SATIRE AND PROTEST

Lies

Telling lies to the young is wrong.
Proving to them that lies are true is wrong.
Telling them that God's in his heaven
and all's well with the world is wrong.
The young know what you mean. The young are people.
Tell them the difficulties can't be counted,
and let them see not only what will be
but see with clarity these present times.
Say obstacles exist they must encounter
sorrow happens, hardship happens.
The hell with it. Who never knew
the price of happiness will not be happy.
Forgive no error you recognise,
it will repeat itself, increase,
and afterwards our pupils
will not forgive in us what we forgave.

Y. YEVTUSHENKO
(*trans. R. Milner-Gulland and P. Levi, S.J.*)

Prayer of a Black Boy

Lord, I am so tired.
Tired I entered this world.
Far have I wandered since the cock crew,
And the road to school is steep.
Lord, I do not want to go into their school,
Please help me that I need not go again.
I want to follow father into the cool gorges.
When the night is hovering over magic forests
Where spirits play before dawn.
Barefoot, I want to tread the red-hot paths,
That boil in midday sun.
And then lie down to sleep beneath a Mango tree.

And I want to wake up only
When down there the white man's siren starts to howl,
And the factory,
A ship on the sugarfields,
Lands and spits its crew
Of black workers into the landscape . . .
Lord, I do not want to go into their school,
Please help me that I need not go again,
It's true, they say a little negro ought to go,
So that he might become
Just like the gentlemen of the city,
So that he might become a real gentleman.
But I, I do not want to become
A gentleman of the city, or as they call it
A real gentleman.
I'd rather stroll along the sugar stores
Where the tight sacks are piled
With brown sugar, brown like my skin.
I'd rather listen – when the moon is whispering
Tenderly into the ear of cocopalms,
To what the old man who always smokes
Recites with breaking voice during the night,
The stories of Samba and Master Hare
And many others more that are not found in any book.
Lord, the negroes have had too much work already,
Why should we learn again from foreign books,
About all kinds of things we've never seen?
And then, their school is far too sad,
Just as sad as these gentlemen of the city,
These real gentlemen
Who do not even know how to dance by the light of the moon,
Who do not even know how to walk on the flesh of their feet,
Who do not even know how to tell the tales of their fathers
By the light of their nightly fires.
O Lord, I do not want to go into their schools again.

GUY TIROLIEN

Telephone Conversation

The price seemed reasonable, location
Indifferent. The landlady swore she lived
Off premises. Nothing remained
But self-confession. 'Madam,' I warned,
'I hate a wasted journey – I am African.'
Silence. Silenced transmission of
Pressurized good-breeding. Voice, when it came,
Lipstick coated, long gold-rolled
Cigarette-holder pipped. Caught I was, foully.
'HOW DARK?' . . . I had not misheard. . . . 'ARE YOU LIGHT
OR VERY DARK?' Button B. Button A. Stench
Of rancid breath of public hide-and-speak.
Red booth. Red pillar-box. Red double-tiered
Omnibus squelching tar. It *was* real! Shamed
By ill-mannered silence, surrender
Pushed dumbfounded to beg simplification.
Considerate she was, varying the emphasis –
'ARE YOU DARK? OR VERY LIGHT?' Revelation came.
'You mean – like plain or milk chocolate?'
Her assent was clinical, crushing in its light
Impersonality. Rapidly, wave-length adjusted,
I chose. 'West African sepia' – and as afterthought,
'Down in my passport.' Silence for spectroscopic
Flight of fancy, till truthfulness clanged her accent
Hard on the mouthpiece. 'WHAT'S THAT?' conceding
'DON'T KNOW WHAT THAT IS.' 'Like brunette.'
'THAT'S DARK, ISN'T IT?' 'Not altogether.
Facially, I am brunette, but madam, you should see
The rest of me. Palm of my hand, soles of my feet
Are a peroxide blonde. Friction, caused –
Foolishly madam – by sitting down, has turned
My bottom raven black – One moment madam!' – sensing
Her receiver rearing on the thunderclap
About my ears – 'Madam,' I pleaded, 'wouldn't you rather
See for yourself?'   WOLE SOYINKA

Girl with a doll, Washington. *Photo: Constantine Manos*

101

ygUDuh

     ydoan
     yunnuhstan

     ydoan o
     yunnuhstan dem
     yguduh ged

     yunnuhstan dem doidee
     yguduh ged riduh
     ydoan o nudn
LISN bud LISN

        dem
        gud
        am

        lidl yelluh bas
        tuds weer goin

duhSIVILEYEzum

        e. e. cummings

Refugee Blues

Say this city has ten million souls,
Some are living in mansions, some are living in holes:
Yet there's no place for us, my dear, yet there's no place for us.

Once we had a country and we thought it fair,
Look in the atlas and you'll find it there:
We cannot go there now, my dear, we cannot go there now.

In the village churchyard there grows an old yew,
Every spring it blossoms anew:
Old passports can't do that, my dear, old passports can't do that.

The consul banged the table and said :
'If you've got no passport you're officially dead' :
But we are still alive, my dear, but we are still alive.

Went to a committee; they offered me a chair;
Asked me politely to return next year :
But where shall we go today, my dear, but where shall we go
    today?

Came to a public meeting; the speaker got up and said :
'If we let them in, they will steal our daily bread';
He was talking of you and me, my dear, he was talking of you
    and me.

Thought I heard the thunder rumbling in the sky;
It was Hitler over Europe, saying : 'They must die';
O we were in his mind, my dear, O we were in his mind.

Saw a poodle in a jacket fastened with a pin,
Saw a door opened and a cat let in :
But they weren't German Jews, my dear, but they weren't
    German Jews.

Went down to the harbour and stood upon the quay,
Saw the fish swimming as if they were free :
Only ten feet away, my dear, only ten feet away.

Walked through a wood, saw the birds in the trees;
They had no politicians and sang at their ease :
They weren't the human race, my dear, they weren't the human
    race.

Dreamed I saw a building with a thousand floors,
A thousand windows and a thousand doors;
Not one of them was ours, my dears, not one of them was ours.

Stood on a great plain in the falling snow;
Ten thousand soldiers marched to and fro :
Looking for you and me, my dear, looking for you and me.

W. H. AUDEN

Algerian Refugee Camp
Aïn-Khemouda

You have black eyes,
Four years of age,
A chic, cast-off coat
– pepper-and-salt, double-breasted –
A label naming you 'Mohammed',
Some slippers, a squashed felt hat.
Nothing else. And 'nothing' means just that.

This camp is your home until – well, until.
A flag flaps on a hill.
The *oued* soon will be dry;
Do you know how to cry?

Smoke curls from the tents
Where women who are not your mother,
Hennaed and trinketed, cook.
Your eyes see but do not look.
And men who are not your father,
Turbaned and burned, sit stiff
In rows, like clay pigeons, on a cliff.
Targets do not easily relax.
Your hair is fair as flax.

Guns rattle the mauve hills
Where the last warmth spills
On villages where once you were
One of a family that died.
Not much else. Just that.

You pull down the brim of your hat.
Who knows what goes on inside?

ALAN ROSS

104

A Beautiful Young Nymph Going to Bed

Written for the honour of the fair sex

Corinna, pride of Drury-lane,
For whom no shepherd sighs in vain;
Never did Covent-Garden boast
So bright a batter'd strolling toast!
No drunken rake to pick her up;
No cellar where on tick to sup;
Returning at the midnight hour,
Four stories climbing to her bower;
Then, seated on a three-legg'd chair,
Takes off her artificial hair;
Now picking out a crystal eye,
She wipes it clean and lays it by.
Her eyebrows from a mouse's hide
Stuck on with art on either side,
Pulls off with care, and first displays 'em,
Then in a play-book smoothly lays 'em,
Now dextrously her plumpers draws,
That serve to fill her hollow jaws,
Untwists a wire, and from her gums
A set of teeth completely comes;
Proceeding on, the lovely goddess
Unlaces next her steel-ribb'd bodice,
Which, by the operator's skill,
Press down the lumps, the hollows fill.
Up goes her hand and off she slips
The bolsters that supply her hips.
But must, before she goes to bed,
Rub off the daubs of white and red,
And smooth the furrows in her front
With greasy paper stuck upon't.
She takes a bolus* ere she sleeps;   *a large pill
And then between two blankets creeps.

JONATHAN SWIFT

105

From The Rape of the Lock

And now, unveil'd, the Toilet stands display'd,
Each Silver Vase in mystic Order laid.
First, rob'd in White, the Nymph intent adores
With Head uncover'd, the Cosmetic Pow'rs.
And heav'nly Image in the Glass appears,
To that she bends, to that her Eyes she rears;
Th'inferior Priestess, at her Altar's side,
Trembling, begins the sacred Rites of Pride.
Unnumber'd Treasures ope at once, and here
The various Off'rings of the World appear;
From each she nicely culls with curious Toil,
And decks the Goddess with the glitt'ring Spoil.
This Casket India's glowing Gems unlocks,
And all Arabia breathes from yonder Box.
The Tortoise here and Elephant unite,
Transform'd to Combs, the speckled and the white.
Here Files of Pins extend their shining Rows,
Puffs, Powders, Patches, Bibles, Billet-doux.
Now awful Beauty puts on all its Arms;
The Fair each moment rises in her Charms,
Repairs her Smiles, awakens ev'ry Grace,
And calls forth all the Wonders of her Face;
Sees by Degrees a purer Blush arise,
And keener Lightnings quicken in her Eyes.
The busy Sylphs surround their darling Care;
These set the Head, and those divide the Hair,
Some fold the Sleeve, whilst others plait the Gown;
And Betty's prais'd for Labours not her own.

ALEXANDER POPE

How Beastly the Bourgeois Is

How beastly the bourgeois is
especially the male of the species –

Presentable eminently presentable –
shall I make you a present of him?

Isn't he handsome? isn't he healthy? Isn't he a fine specimen?
doesn't he look the fresh clean englishman, outside?
Isn't it god's own image? tramping his thirty miles a day
after partridges, or a little rubber ball?
wouldn't you like to be like that, well off, and quite the thing?

Oh, but wait!
Let him meet a new emotion, let him be faced with another
      man's need,
let him come home to a bit of moral difficulty, let life face him
      with a new demand on his understanding
and then watch him go soggy, like a wet meringue.
Watch him turn into a mess, either a fool or a bully.
Just watch the display of him, confronted with a new demand
      on his intelligence,
a new life-demand.

How beastly the bourgeois is
especially the male of the species –

Nicely groomed, like a mushroom
standing there so sleek and erect and eyeable –
and like a fungus, living on the remains of bygone life
sucking his life out of the dead leaves of greater life than
      his own.

And even so, he's stale, he's been there too long.
Touch him, and you'll find he's all gone inside
just like an old mushroom, all wormy inside, and hollow
under a smooth skin and an upright appearance.

[Youth against the bomb. *Photo: Philip Jones Griffiths*

107

Full of seething, wormy, hollow feelings
rather nasty –
How beastly the bourgeois is!

Standing in their thousands, these appearances, in damp
    England
what a pity they can't all be kicked over
like sickening toadstools, and left to melt back, swiftly
into the soil of England.

D. H. LAWRENCE

Geriatric Ward

Feeding time in the geriatric ward;
I wondered how they found their mouths,
and seeing that not one looked up, inquired
'Do they have souls?'

'If I had a machine-gun,' answered the doctor
'I'd show you dignity in death instead of living death.
Death wasn't meant to be kept alive.
But we're under orders
to pump blood and air in after the mind's gone.
I don't understand souls;
I only learned about cells
law-abiding as leaves
withering under frost.
But we, never handing over
to Mother who knows best,
spray cabbages with oxygen, hoping for a smile,
count pulses of breathing bags whose direction is lost,
and think we've won.

Here's a game you can't win –
One by one they ooze away in the cold.
There's no society forbidding
this dragged-out detention of the old.'

PHOEBE HESKETH

Base Details

If I were fierce, and bald, and short of breath,
   I'd live with scarlet Majors at the Base,
And speed glum heroes up the line to death.
   You'd see me with my puffy petulant face,
Guzzling and gulping in the best hotel,
   Reading the Roll of Honour. 'Poor young chap,'
I'd say – 'I used to know his father well;
   Yes, we've lost heavily in this last scrap.'
And when the war is done and youth stone dead,
I'd toddle safely home and die – in bed.

SIEGFRIED SASSOON

'They'

The Bishop tells us: 'When the boys come back
'They will not be the same; for they'll have fought
'In a just cause: they lead the last attack
'On Anti-Christ; their comrades' blood has bought
'New right to breed an honourable race,
'They have challenged Death and dared him face to face.'

'We're none of us the same!' the boys reply.
'For George lost both his legs; and Bill's stone blind;
'Poor Jim's shot through the lungs and like to die;
'And Bert's gone syphilitic: you'll not find
'A chap who's served that hasn't found *some* change.'
And the Bishop said: 'The ways of God are strange!'

SIEGFRIED SASSOON

Epitaph On A Dead Statesman

I could not dig: I dared not rob:
Therefore I lied to please the mob.
Now all my lies are proved untrue
And I must face the men I slew.
What tale shall serve me here among
Mine angry and defrauded young?

RUDYARD KIPLING

A Protest in the Sixth Year of Ch'ien Fu (AD 879)

The hills and rivers of the lowland country
    You have made your battle-ground.
How do you suppose the people who live there
    Will procure 'firewood and hay'?*   * the necessities of life
Do not let me hear you talking together
    About titles and promotions;
For a single general's reputation
    Is made out of ten thousand corpses.

TS'AO SUNG (*trans. Arthur Waley*)

*Above the uniform is situated a head for the soldier to know how
high the hand has to be lifted to make a salute.*

Cartoon: Bruno Paul

Discussion and Writing

In the course of your reading you will have noticed groups of poems in this section which protest against such things as colour prejudice, war, the refugee problem, female vanity or the way in which society treats its old people. Some of these protests are direct; many of them adopt a satirical tone. Before you write, remind yourself what the word 'satire' means by discussing the following questions:

What motives does the satirist have in writing?
What techniques does he use?
What aim has he in view?

1 The two poems on pages 98 to 101 deal with one of the major issues of our time, the colour problem. Each poem treats a different aspect of this problem and it is worth spending some time talking about the experiences and feelings of the Africans in each case. What are the causes of colour prejudice?

In the course of your discussion, particularly of Wole Soyinka's poem which dramatises a conversation between an English landlady and a Nigerian, you may well draw upon your own knowledge and experience of coloured people in this country and the problems they face. You may be able to dramatise an encounter between white and black, or to write about an incident you have seen which has stuck in your memory, or write a poem which expresses some ideas about an aspect of the colour problem over which you feel strongly. The photograph on p. 100 may help.

2 Minority groups within any society usually provoke strong reactions in the rest of the public either in support of, or, more commonly, against their beliefs and behaviour. You may have felt indignant (either at the minority group or at society's treatment of it) about 'hippies', 'skinheads', or gypsies.

Perhaps you could put your protest into words. The picture on p. 108 may suggest some ideas here.

3 Look at Bruno Paul's satirical portrait of the two soldiers and his caption on p. 113. What is the artist attacking through this satire?

A second picture on p. 96 shows us a live situation: the reaction of a young protester when confronted by a line of equally young guardsmen during the 1967 Peace March on the Pentagon in Washington.

Look at both these pictures carefully and, after discussing their implications, perhaps you will find some ideas you would like to examine in greater depth in a poem.

4 Read again Phoebe Hesketh's *Geriatric Ward* on p. 110, Sassoon's war poems on p. 111, and the two poems about refugees on pp. 102 to 104. All of them, in different ways, are responses to society's indifference to suffering. There may be some area of human life where you have been aware of society turning its back on suffering. Perhaps a local situation – a pensioner, living alone, barely able to cope with the necessities of daily living; or, perhaps, an international situation where governments seem to do insufficient to relieve the miseries of the oppressed, the destitute and the starving. You may find ideas for a protest poem here.

5 Pretence, hypocrisy, pride, people affecting to be what they are not are common objects of the satirist's mockery as the poems on pp. 105 to 107 show. If you know of any examples of this sort of behaviour perhaps you could write a satirical portrait in free verse as Lawrence does or in rhyming couplets as Swift and Pope do.

6 In previous books in this series we have printed *parodies* of various poems, where the style of a particular poem is imitated but the content is made to seem absurd. You may remember John Betjeman's parody of a hymn which begins 'We spray the fields and scatter the poison on the ground'. This kind of attack can be a most effective form of protest. Perhaps you could attempt something similar, for example, a school song, if you have one, or end of term songs or hymns.

Another similar possibility might be to parody the inanities of advertising jingles or to produce your own pop song parodying the more absurd side of some pop lyrics.

7 Linked closely to the previous suggestion is the question that many pupils of your own age raise. How far does the image of the institution you are in, the way in which it sees itself and in which it would like itself to be seen, match the reality of what it is like to you as one of its members? Are its traditions, its rules and outlook worth something or not? Do you feel strongly enough to write on any aspect of its daily life? Here are a few ideas that might provoke a poem of protest or satire – assemblies, prize-giving or speech day, prefects, 'the school spirit', games, loyalty to the school, uniform. You can probably add many more.

FAMILY

Morning Song

Love set you going like a fat gold watch.
The midwife slapped your footsoles, and your bald cry
Took its place among the elements.

Our voices echo, magnifying your arrival. New statue.
In a drafty museum, your nakedness
Shadows our safety. We stand round blankly as walls.

I'm no more your mother
Than the cloud that distils a mirror to reflect its own slow
Effacement at the wind's hand.

All night your moth-breath
Flickers among the flat pink roses. I wake to listen:
A far sea moves in my ear.

One cry, and I stumble from bed, cow-heavy and floral
In my Victorian nightgown.
Your mouth opens clean as a cat's. The window square

Whitens and swallows its dull stars. And now you try
Your handful of notes;
The clear vowels rise like balloons.

SYLVIA PLATH

116

Baby Running Barefoot

When the white feet of the baby beat across the grass
The little white feet nod like white flowers in a wind,
They poise and run like puffs of wind that pass
Over water where the weeds are thinned.

And the sight of their white playing in the grass
Is winsome as a robin's song, so fluttering:
Or like two butterflies that settle on a glass
Cup for a moment, soft little wing-beats uttering.

And I wish that the baby would tack across here to me
Like a wind-shadow running on a pond, so she could stand
With two little bare white feet upon my knee
And I could feel her feet in either hand

Cool as syringa buds in morning hours,
Or firm and silken as young peony flowers.

D. H. LAWRENCE

A Child Half-asleep

Stealthily parting the small-hours silence,
a hardly-embodied figment of his brain
comes down to sit with me
as I work late.
Flat-footed, as though his legs and feet
were still asleep.

On a stool,
staring into the fire,
his dummy dangling.

Fire ignites the small coals of his eyes;
it stares back through the holes
into his head, into the darkness.

'Rocking Chair No. 2', *Henry Moore*

I ask what woke him.

'A wolf dreamed me,' he says.

TONY CONNOR

The Almond Tree

I

All the way to the hospital
the lights were green as peppermints.
Trees of black iron broke into leaf
ahead of me, as if
I were the lucky prince
in an enchanted wood
summoning summer with my whistle,
banishing winter with a nod.

Swung by the road from bend to bend,
I was aware that blood was running
down through the delta of my wrist
and under arches
of bright bone. Centuries,
continents it had crossed;
from an undisclosed beginning
spiralling to an unmapped end.

II

Crossing (at sixty) Magdalen Bridge
Let it be a son, a son, said
the man in the driving mirror,
Let it be a son. The tower
held up its hand : the college
bells shook their blessing on his head.

III

I parked in an almond's
shadow blossom, for the tree
was waving, waving me
upstairs with a child's hands.

IV

Up
the spinal stair
and at the top
along
a bone-white corridor
the blood tide swung
me swung me to a room
whose walls shuddered
with the shuddering womb.
Under the sheet
wave after wave, wave
after wave beat
on the bone coast, bringing
ashore – whom?
New –
minted, my bright farthing!
Coined by our love, stamped with
our images, how you
enrich us! Both
you make one. Welcome
to your white sheet,
my best poem!

V

At seven-thirty
the visitors' bell
scissored the calm
of the corridors.
The doctor walked with me
to the slicing doors.

His hand upon my arm,
his voice – *I have to tell
you* – set another bell
beating in my head :
your son is a mongol
the doctor said.

VI

How easily the word went in –
clean as a bullet
leaving no mark on the skin,
stopping the heart within it.

This was my first death.
The 'I' ascending on a slow
last thermal breath
studied the man below
as a pilot treading air might
the buckled shell of his plane –
boot, glove, and helmet
feeling no pain

from the snapped wires' radiant ends.
Looking down from a thousand feet
I held four walls in the lens
of an eye; wall, window, the street

a torrent of windscreens, my own
car under its almond tree,
and the almond waving me down.
I wrestled against gravity,

but light was melting and the gulf
cracked open. Unfamiliar
the body of my late self
I carried to the car.

121

VII

The hospital – its heavy freight
lashed down ship-shape ward over ward –
steamed into night with some on board
soon to be lost if the desperate

charts were known. Others would come
altered to land or find the land
altered. At their voyage's end
some would be added to, some

diminished. In a numbered cot
my son sailed from me : never to come
ashore into my kingdom
speaking my language. Better not

look that way. The almond tree
was beautiful in labour. Blood –
dark, quickening, bud after bud
split, flower after flower shook free.

On the darkening wind a pale
face floated. Out of reach. Only when
the buds, all the buds, were broken
would the tree be in full sail.

In labour the tree was becoming
itself. I, too, rooted in earth
and ringed by darkness, from the death
of myself saw myself blossoming.

wrenched from the caul of my thirty
years' growing, fathered by my son,
unkindly in a kind season
by love shattered and set free.

VIII

You turn to the window for the first time.
I am called to the cot
to see your focus shift,
take tendril-hold on a shaft
of sun, explore its dusty surface, climb
to an eye you cannot

meet. You have a sickness they cannot heal
the doctors say : locked in
your body you will remain.
Well, I have been locked in mine.
We will tunnel each other out. You seal
the covenant with a grin.

In the days we have known one another,
my little mongol love,
I have learnt more from your lips
than you will from mine perhaps :
I have learnt that to live is to suffer,
to suffer is to live.

JON STALLWORTHY

Death of a Son

(who died in a mental hospital, aged one)

Something has ceased to come along with me.
Something like a person : something very like one.
    And there was no nobility in it
        Or anything like that.

Something was there like a one-year-
Old house, dumb as stone. While the near buildings
    Sang like birds and laughed
        Understanding the pact

They were to have with silence. But he
Neither sang nor laughed. He did not bless silence
Like bread, with words.
He did not forsake silence.

But rather, like a house in mourning
Kept the eye turned to watch the silence while
The other houses like birds
Sang around him.

And the breathing silence neither
Moved nor was still.

I have seen stones : I have seen brick
But this house was made up of neither bricks nor stone
But a house of flesh and blood
With flesh of stone

And bricks for blood. A house
Of stones and blood in breathing silence with the other
Birds singing crazy on its chimneys.
But this was silence,

This was something else, this was
Hearing and speaking though he was a house drawn
Into silence, this was
Something religious in his silence,

Something shining in his quiet,
This was different this was altogether something else :
Though he never spoke, this
Was something to do with death.

And then slowly the eye stopped looking
Inward. The silence rose and became still.
The look turned to the outer place and stopped,
With the birds still shrilling around him.
And as if he could speak

He turned over on his side with this one year
Red as a wound
He turned over as if he could be sorry for this
And out of his eyes two great tears rolled, like stones,
                    and he died.

JON SILKIN

For My Son

Not ever to talk when merely requested,
Not ever to be the performing child,
This is what you would establish;
                    always keeping
Private and awkward counsel against
All coaxing; and going – one hopes –
The way of a good will,

To your own true designs. Which is
The way of some human institutions,
Growing not as any collective urge
                    would have them
(In its own placable image) but into
Their own more wayward value – strong,
Untidy, original, self-possessed.

ALAN BROWNJOHN

Piano

Softly, in the dusk, a woman is singing to me;
Taking me back down the vista of years, till I see
A child sitting under the piano, in the boom of the tingling
    strings
And pressing the small, poised feet of a mother who smiles
    as she sings.

In spite of myself, the insidious mastery of song
Betrays me back, till the heart of me weeps to belong
To the old Sunday evenings at home, with winter outside
And hymns in the cosy parlour, the tinkling piano our guide.

So now it is vain for the singer to burst into clamour
With the great black piano appassionato. The glamour
Of childish days is upon me, my manhood is cast
Down in the flood of remembrance, I weep like a child for
    the past.

D. H. LAWRENCE

Paternal Instruction

Children, I am training you now
to carry out the only favour
I will ever ask you. Children,
I am working for the day when
all the slaps and shouts are
cancelled out. Children, obey me.

I don't know for sure when
I will expect you to perform
this service. Let's say I'll
live for three score years and ten
and am exactly half way there.

So this is, in fact, a semi-anniversary;
the point at which your lesson
should begin. Andrea, say after me:
'In my teenage days I hated him,
but later saw a core of good intent.
At all events, I remembered him:
his name was Edwin and he lived.'

Nicholas say: 'He was never
a perfect father: too authoritarian;
liable to shout loudly and retire
to a quiet corner with a book.
I remember the look of him:
his name was Edwin and he lived.'

I am trusting you to repeat these
things, daily, for the remainder
of your lives. And, later, to
teach your baby-sister
something similar to say.

I do not expect my discipline
to extend to the training of
your children. When you die
I will accept the end: will
open my mouth and let the crawling
kingdom enter, and give my face
leave to crumble from my head.

EDWIN BROCK

Afternoons

Summer is fading:
The leaves fall in ones and twos
From trees bordering
The new recreation ground.
In the hollows of afternoons
Young mothers assemble
At swing and sandpit
Setting free their children.

Behind them, at intervals,
Stand husbands in skilled trades,
An estateful of washing,
And the albums, lettered
Our Wedding, lying
Near the television:
Before them, the wind
Is ruining their courting-places

That are still courting-places
(but the lovers are all in school),
And their children, so intent on
Finding more unripe acorns,
Expect to be taken home.
Their beauty has thickened.
Something is pushing them
To the side of their own lives.
                    PHILIP LARKIN

My Grandmother

She kept an antique shop – or it kept her.
Among Apostle spoons and Bristol glass,
The faded silks, the heavy furniture,
She watched her own reflection in the brass
Salvers and silver bowls, as if to prove
Polish was all, there was no need of love.

And I remember how I once refused
To go out with her, since I was afraid.
It was perhaps a wish not to be used
Like antique objects. Though she never said
That she was hurt, I still could feel the guilt
Of that refusal, guessing how she felt.

Later, too frail to keep a shop, she put
All her best things in one long narrow room.
The place smelt old, of things too long kept shut,
The smell of absences where shadows come
That can't be polished. There was nothing then
To give her own reflection back again.

And when she died I felt no grief at all,
Only the guilt of what I once refused.
I walked into her room among the tall
Sideboards and cupboards – things she never used
But needed : and no finger-marks were there,
Only the new dust falling through the air.

ELIZABETH JENNINGS

Heredity

I am the family face;
Flesh perishes, I live on,
Projecting trait and trace
Through time to times anon,
And leaping from place to place
Over oblivion.

The years-heired feature that can
In curve and voice and eye
Despise the human span
Of durance – that is I;
The eternal thing in man,
That heeds no call to die.

THOMAS HARDY

Discussion and Writing

1 In one of his plays Oscar Wilde wrote 'Children begin by loving their parents; after a time they judge them; rarely, if ever, do they forgive them.' Does one of these stages approximate to your feelings for your own parents? If so, what do you really mean by 'loving', 'judging' or 'forgiving'? Perhaps you could examine what people's feelings are for their mother and father and write about them, choosing either a real or an imaginary situation.

2 Pages 116 to 125 contain several poems and a photograph of a sculpture by Henry Moore all of which are concerned with the relationship between either a mother or a father and very young children. Are you able to describe, from reading through these pages, some of the feelings which parents have for their babies and youngsters?

What are the demands made by young children emotionally and physically?

What might be the rewards from the parents' point of view?

Perhaps an idea for a poem will be suggested by your discussion.

3 Elizabeth Jennings' poem on p. 129 describes the writer's strangely mixed feelings for her grandmother. Are there any points in the

poem where you feel that your experience has been similar to that of Elizabeth Jennings?

In what ways does your relationship with your parents differ from that between you and your grandparents?

If you feel that there is a poem here perhaps it is a good idea to build up a picture of your grandmother or grandfather – maybe through the objects, furniture and rooms with which you associate them, for old people, particularly, seem to project their personalities into their immediate surroundings.

4 You may be aware of "parents' jargon" when your mother or father is talking to you. How often have you been made to feel that:

they are 'just trying to bring you up properly'
you need 'a bit more discipline'
you don't 'work hard enough'
you 'shouldn't go around with *that* gang'
'It wasn't like this when I was young'
'When I was your age we were never allowed . . . '

Often there is an unnecessary friction between the generations which is caught in such phrases. Imagine yourself involved in a tricky conversation with your parents and try to write down the stream of thoughts, feelings and comments which you have. Alternatively, you could put yourself in the rôle of parent and attempt the same thing from their point of view.

5 Although most families have certain things in common, all families are unique. Try to capture the atmosphere of your family group engaged on some activity in which all the members are involved. You might, for example, describe an annual family gathering at Christmas or when numerous relations are assembled for a celebration of some kind, or perhaps just your immediate family sitting watching television, at breakfast, or on the beach.

6 Some of you may have no brothers or sisters, others might wonder what this is like. Perhaps you could write a poem with the title 'The only child'.

7 One's feelings for brothers or sisters are very variable and arguments will arise from time to time. You may, for example, feel that a much younger or older child than yourself is given different treatment by your parents. Perhaps you can find an idea for an original piece of writing here, either in the description of such an argument or in trying to crystallise your feelings about your brother or sister.

WORK

Toads

Why should I let the toad *work*
   Squat on my life?
Can't I use my wit as a pitchfork
   And drive the brute off?

Six days of the week it soils
   With its sickening poison –
Just for paying a few bills!
   That's out of proportion.

Lots of folk live on their wits:
   Lecturers, lispers,
Losels, loblolly-men, louts –
   They don't end as paupers;

Lots of folk live up lanes
   With fires in a bucket,
Eat windfalls and tinned sardines –
   They seem to like it.

Their nippers have got bare feet,
   Their unspeakable wives
Are skinny as whippets – and yet
   No one actually *starves*.

Ah, were I courageous enough
   To shout, *Stuff your pension!*
But I know, all too well, that's the stuff
   That dreams are made on:

For something sufficiently toad-like
    Squats in me too;
Its hunkers are heavy as hard luck,
    And cold as snow,

And will never allow me to blarney
    My way to getting
The fame and the girl and the money
    All at one sitting.

I don't say, one bodies the other
    One's spiritual truth;
But I do say it's hard to lose either,
    When you have both.

PHILIP LARKIN

Song of the Wagondriver

My first love was the ten-ton truck
they gave me when I started,
and though she played the bitch with me
I grieved when we were parted.

Since then I've had a dozen more,
the wound was quick to heal,
and now it's easier to say
I'm married to my wheel.

I've trunked it north, I've trunked it south,
on wagons good and bad,
but none were ever really like
the first I ever had.

The life is hard, the hours are long,
sometimes I cease to feel,
but I go on, for it seems to me
I'm married to my wheel.

'The Builders', *Fernand Léger*

Often I think of my home and kids,
out on the road at night,
and think of taking a local job
provided the money's right.

Two nights a week I see my wife,
and eat a decent meal,
but otherwise, for all my life,
I'm married to my wheel.

B. S. JOHNSON

Morning Work

A gang of labourers on the piled wet timber
That shines blood-red beside the railway siding
Seem to be making out of the blue of the morning
Something faery and fine, the shuttles sliding.

The red-gold spools of their hands and their faces swinging
Hither and thither across the high crystalline frame
Of day: trolls at the cave of ringing cerulean mining
And laughing with labour, living their work like a game.

D. H. LAWRENCE

Work

There is no point in work
unless it absorbs you
like an absorbing game.

If it doesn't absorb you
if it's never any fun,
don't do it.

When a man goes out into his work
he is alive like a tree in spring,
he is living, not merely working.

D. H. LAWRENCE

Wreath Makers: Leeds Market

A cocksure boy in the gloom of the gilded market bends
With blunt fingers a bow of death, and the flowers work with
   him.
They fashion a grave of grass with dead bracken and fine ferns.

An old woman with a mouthful of wires and a clutch of irises
Mourns in perpetual black, and her fists with the sunken rings
Rummage in the fragrant workbasket of a wreath.

A laughing Flora dangles a cross between her thighs
Like a heavy child, feeds it with pale plump lilies, crimson
Roses, wraps it in greenery and whips it with wires.

And here a grieving flower god with a lyre in his arms
Fumbles mute strings in the rough-gentle machine of his fingers,
His eyes wet violets, and in his mouth a last carnation. . . .

Mourners all, they know not why they mourn,
But work and breathe the perfumes of their trade
(Those flower-vines, through which death more keenly speaks)

With suitable dispassion; though they know their emblems fade,
And they at last must bear a yellowed wreath
That other hands, and other harvesters have made.

                                        JAMES KIRKUP

Stripping Walls

I have been practical as paint today, wholesome
    as bread –
I have stripped walls. I rose early and felt
    clean-limbed
And steady-eyed and said 'Today I will strip
    those walls.'
I have not been chewing my nails and gazing
    through windows
And grovelling for a subject or happiness. There
    was the subject.
Simple and tall. And when the baker called he
    was civil
And looking at me with some respect he said
'I see you're stripping walls' – I could see he
    liked me.
And when I opened the door to the greengrocer,
    I glinted my eyes
And leaned nonchalantly and poked some toma-
    toes and said as an aside
'I'm stripping walls today.' 'Are you?' he asked,
    interested, and I said
'Yes, just stripping those walls.' I could feel my
    forearms thicken, grow
Hairy, and when the laundry arrived I met it
    with rolled sleeves.
'Stripping walls?' he asked. 'Yeah,' I said, as if it
    were unimportant,
'Stripping walls. You know.' He nodded and
    smiled as if he knew.
And with a step like a spring before the meal I
    strode
Down to the pub and leaned and sipped ale and
    heard them talk
How one had cleared land that morning, another
    chopped wood.

When an eye caught mine I winked and flipped
    my head. 'I've been
Stripping walls,' I said. 'Have you?' 'Yeah, you
    know, just stripping.'
They nodded. 'Can be tricky,' one mumbled. I
    nodded. 'It can be that.'
'Plaster,' another said. 'Holes,' I said. 'Work-
    manship,' said another
And shook his head. 'Yeah, have a drink,' I said.
And whistled through the afternoon, and stood
    once or twice
At the door-jamb, the stripper dangling from my
    fingers.
'Stripping?' asked passing neighbours. I nodded
    and they went on happy –
They were happy that I was stripping walls. It
    meant a lot.

When it grew dark, I went out for the freshness,
    'Hey!' I called up,
'I've been stripping walls!' 'Just fancy that!'
    answered the moon with
A long pale face like Hopkins. 'Hey fellers!'
    he called to the stars,
'This little hairy runt has been stripping walls!'
    'Bully for him,' chimed
The Pole star, remote and cool as Virgil, 'He's a
    good, good lad.'
I crept to the kitchen, pursued by celestial
    laughter
'You've done well today,' she said. 'Shall we
    paint tomorrow?'
'Ah, shut up!' I said, and started hacking my
    nails.

BRIAN JONES

Mending Wall

Something there is that doesn't love a wall,
That sends the frozen-ground-swell under it,
And spills the upper boulders in the sun;
And makes gaps even two can pass abreast.
The work of hunters is another thing:
I have come after them and made repair
Where they have left not one stone on a stone,
But they would rather have the rabbit out of hiding,
To please the yelping dogs. The gaps I mean,
No one has seen them made or heard them made,
But at spring mending-time we find them there.
I let my neighbour know beyond the hill;
And on a day we meet to walk the line
And set the wall between us once again.
We keep the wall between us as we go.
To each the boulders that have fallen to each.
And some are loaves and some so nearly balls
We have to use a spell to make them balance:
'Stay where you are until our backs are turned!'
We wear our fingers rough with handling them.
Oh, just another kind of outdoor game,
One on a side. It comes to little more:
There where it is we do not need the wall:
He is all pine and I am apple orchard.
My apple trees will never get across
And eat the cones under his pines, I tell him.
He only says, 'Good fences make good neighbours.'
Spring is the mischief in me, and I wonder
If I could put a notion in his head:
'Why do they make good neighbours? Isn't it
Where there are cows? But here there are no cows.
Before I built a wall I'd ask to know
What I was walling in or walling out,
And to whom I was like to give offence.
Something there is that doesn't love a wall,
That wants it down'. I could say 'Elves' to him,

But it's not elves exactly, and I'd rather
He said it for himself. I see him there
Bringing a stone grasped firmly by the top
In each hand, like an old-stone savage armed.
He moves in darkness as it seems to me,
Not of woods only and the shade of trees.
He will not go behind his father's saying,
And he likes having thought of it so well
He says again, 'Good fences make good neighbours.'

ROBERT FROST

The Wife's Tale

When I had spread it all on linen cloth
Under the hedge, I called them over.
The hum and gulp of the thresher ran down
And the big belt slewed to a standstill, straw
Hanging undelivered in the jaws.
There was such quiet that I heard their boots
Crunching the stubble twenty yards away.

He lay down and said 'Give these fellows theirs.
I'm in no hurry,' plucking grass in handfuls
And tossing it in the air. 'That looks well.'
(He nodded at my white cloth on the grass.)
'I declare a woman could lay out a field
Though boys like us have little call for cloths.'
He winked, then watched me as I poured a cup
And buttered the thick slices that he likes.
'It's threshing better than I thought, and mind
It's good clean seed. Away over there and look.'
Always this inspection has to be made
Even when I don't know what to look for.

Potter. *Photo: Neville Cooper*

But I ran my hand in the half-filled bags
Hooked to the slots. It was hard as shot,
Innumerable and cool. The bags gaped
Where the chutes ran back to the stilled drum
And forks were stuck at angles in the ground
As javelins might mark lost battlefields.
I moved between them back across the stubble.

They lay in the ring of their own crusts and dregs
Smoking and saying nothing. 'There's good yield,
Isn't there?' – as proud as if he were the land itself –
'Enough for crushing and for sowing both.'
And that was it. I'd come and he had shown me
So I belonged no further to the work.
I gathered cups and folded up the cloth
And went. But they still kept their ease
Spread out, unbuttoned, grateful, under the trees.

SEAMUS HEANEY

Toads Revisited

Walking around in the park
Should feel better than work :
The lake, the sunshine,
The grass to lie on,

Blurred playground noises
Beyond black-stockinged nurses –
Not a bad place to be.
Yet it doesn't suit me,

Being one of the men
You meet of an afternoon :
Palsied old step-takers,
Hare-eyed clerks with the jitters,

Waxed-fleshed out-patients
Still vague from accidents,
And characters in long coats
Deep in the litter-baskets –

All dodging the toad work
By being stupid or weak.
Think of being them!
Hearing the hours chime,

Watching the bread delivered,
The sun by clouds covered,
The children going home;
Think of being them,

Turning over their failures
By some bed of lobelias,
Nowhere to go but indoors,
No friends but empty chairs –

No, give me my in-tray,
My loaf-haired secretary,
My shall-I-keep-the-call-in-Sir :
What else can I answer,

When the lights come on at four
At the end of another year?
Give me your arm, old toad;
Help me down Cemetery Road.

PHILIP LARKIN

Discussion and Writing

What satisfaction do you expect from a future job? Enjoyment of the work for its own sake? An opportunity to be creative, to express yourself? The chance to be an organiser or administrator? The ability to earn a lot of money? Will you want a job in which you can see immediate, visible results, or will you be happy simply with the knowledge or feeling of doing something worthwhile which frequently shows no measurable results?

Try to sort out your own priorities here and see how they measure up to those of other members of your class.

1 The discussion should have set you thinking about your future, not only in terms of a job, but also about your whole development over the next few years from adolescence to adulthood. If you try to imagine the future, you may have a mental image of certain places or people; you may think of it through a special metaphor – a river, a road, a ladder or a cave; you may associate it with a particular colour. Try to write about your future as you picture it.

2 In Art or Handicraft lessons some of you will have experienced the satisfaction of creating something of your own making out of clay, wood, metal or material. Even if you do not feel very capable in these lessons, you will probably have seen, at some time in your life, a craftsman at work – a man absorbed in a particular task, using his hands, like the potter in the photograph on p. 140. Notice the concentration and care; the feeling of gentle yet firm control which the potter has over the clay; the absence of strain. Perhaps you could write a poem from this picture or, alternatively, describe one of your own attempts to make something with your hands.

3 *Song of the Wagondriver* on p. 133 is one of many modern work songs, some of which have had popular commercial success. Try to write a work song of your own, describing any job which appeals to you. If there is someone in the class who can play a guitar perhaps your song could be set to music and performed.

4 In our advanced industrial society machines are steadily reducing the number of jobs involving heavy manual labour but increasing those which are tedious and repetitive.

   Have you ever watched people on building sites, roadworks or dockyards where real physical effort is needed? Léger's picture of *The Builders* on p. 134 may help you to imagine such a scene.

144

This painting, together with your own knowledge, may suggest ideas to you for a piece of writing. What does the artist seem to say about the relationship between the builders and their work?

Many of you will know something of the boredom of production line jobs in a modern, automated factory – perhaps through taking a temporary job yourself or through talking to older people about their work. Try to imagine a specific job (it would be very helpful to get someone to describe their work to you) and try to describe it *in detail*. What might your thoughts and feelings be as you worked?

5 From time to time everyone becomes involved in work around the home – decorating, car or motor-bike maintenance, gardening and so on. Some of these jobs are enjoyable as hobbies, others are just duties which you may have been pressured into by your parents. There may be one task which you feel something about in one or other of these ways. Describe it carefully and try to record your feelings for it.

6 If you have a part-time job – perhaps doing a newspaper round, or working in a shop, or being a delivery boy – you may feel you could write about your work. Don't forget that it is often the tiny details that you know about through first-hand experience that make for a vivid picture.

7 Try to put yourself imaginatively in another person's place. What is it like to be a bus driver, a nurse, a teacher, a roadsweeper, a bank clerk, or a miner? What things do they notice most about their surroundings? What thoughts pass through their minds as they work?

8 Some of you will have first-hand experience of the effects of a strike, involving members of your own family or many people in your town; all of you will probably have seen films of speeches, mass meetings, demonstrations. Perhaps you could capture the atmosphere of a strike and think about the effect it has on families, individual workers, and what you feel about it.

TOWN AND COUNTRY

Here

Swerving east, from rich industrial shadows
And traffic all night north; swerving through fields
Too thin and thistled to be called meadows,
And now and then a harsh-named halt, that shields
Workmen at dawn; swerving to solitude
Of skies and scarecrows, haystacks, hares and pheasants,
And the widening river's slow presence,
The piled gold clouds, the shining gull-marked mud,

Gathers to the surprise of a large town:
Here domes and statues, spires and cranes cluster
Beside grain-scattered streets, barge-crowded water,
And residents from raw estates, brought down
The dead straight miles by stealing flat-faced trolleys,
Push through plate-glass swing doors to their desires –
Cheap suits, red kitchen-ware, sharp shoes, iced lollies,
Electric mixers, toasters, washers, driers –

A cut-price crowd, urban yet simple, dwelling
Where only salesmen and relations come
Within a terminate and fishy-smelling
Pastoral of ships up streets, the slave museum,
Tattoo-shops, consulates, grim head-scarfed wives;
And out beyond its mortgaged half-built edges
Fast-shadowed wheat-fields, running high as hedges,
Isolate villages, where removed lives

Loneliness clarifies. Here silence stands
Like heat. Here leaves unnoticed thicken,
Hidden weeds flower, neglected waters quicken,
Luminously-peopled air ascends;
And past the poppies bluish neutral distance
Ends the land suddenly beyond a beach
Of shapes and shingle. Here is unfenced existence:
Facing the sun, untalkative, out of reach.

PHILIP LARKIN

Embankment Before Snow

A zinc afternoon. The barges black,
And black the funnels of tugs nosing
Phlegm-coloured waves slap slapping
Stone wharves. A smell of sacking
And soot. Grey chimneys, and statues
Grey with cold, and grey life-belts.
          Now the arthritic gulls,
Seedy with displeasure, crotchet on railings,
Falling with a fat splash on wet bread.
Green is under black in the gardens
Bearing the frozen face of Huskisson,
Statesman, but trees are black all through.
The sun fumes behind mist which rises
To thicken this smoke, make dusk black.
The river, eyed by launches, hangs its cranes
          That grab nothing
But cold black air, aqueous and rotting.

ALAN ROSS

Paddington Canal

A mocking mirror, the black water turns
Tall houses upside down, makes learned men
Walk on their heads in squares of burning light:
Lovers like folded bats hang in a kiss,
Swaying as if a breeze could sever them.
The barges, giant sea-birds fast asleep,
Lie on the surface, moored and motionless;
Then, drowning gently, are drawn down to join
The sunken lovers and the acrobats.
Out of the grim dimensions of a street
Slowly I see another landscape grow
Downwards into a lost reality;
A magic mirror, the black water tells
Of a reversed Atlantis wisely built
To catch and to transform
The wasted substance of our daily acts,
Accommodate our mad and lovely doubles
In a more graceful city timelessly.

MICHAEL HAMBURGER

The Public Garden

Burnished, burned-out, still burning as the year
you lead me to our stamping ground.
The city and the cruising cars surround
the Public Garden. All's alive –
the children crowding home from school at five,
punting a football in the bricky air,
the sailors and their pick-ups under trees
with Latin labels. And the jaded flock
of swanboats paddles to its dock.
The park is drying.
Dead leaves thicken to a ball
inside the basin of a fountain, where

148

the heads of four stone lions stare
and suck on empty fawcets. Night
deepens. From the arched bridge, we see
the shedding park-bound mallards, how they keep
circling and diving in the lanternlight,
searching for something hidden in the muck.
And now the moon, earth's friend, that cared so much
for us, and cared so little, comes again –
always a stranger! As we walk,
it lies like chalk
over the waters. Everything's aground.
Remember summer? Bubbles filled
the fountain, and we splashed. We drowned
in Eden, while Jehovah's grass-green lyre
was rustling all about us in the leaves
that gurgled by us, turning upside down. . . .
The fountain's failing waters flash around
the garden. Nothing catches fire.

ROBERT LOWELL

October in Clowes Park

The day dispossessed of light. At four o'clock
in the afternoon, a sulphurous, manufactured
twilight, smudging the scummed lake's far side,
leant on the park. Sounds, muffled –
as if the lolling muck clogged them at the source –
crawled to the ear. A skyed ball thudded
to ground, a swan leathered its wings by the island.
I stood and watched a water-hen arrow
shutting silver across the sooty mat
of the lake's surface, an earl's lake,
though these fifty years the corporation's,
and what is left of the extensive estate –
a few acres of scruffy, flat land

framing this wet sore in the minds of property agents –
a public park. All else is built on.
Through swags of trees poked the bare backsides
of encircling villas, garages, gardening sheds,
a ring of lights making the park dimmer.
Boys and men shouldering long rods –
all licensed fishers, by their open way –
scuffled the cinders past me, heading for home,
but I stayed on; the dispossessed day
held me, turned me towards the ruined Hall.
Pulsing in that yellow, luminous, murk
(a trick of the eye), the bits of broken pillar
built into banks, the last upright wall,
the stalactite-hung split shells of stables,
seemed likely to find a voice – such pent-in grief
and anger! – or perhaps to explode silently
with force greater than any known to progress,
wiping the district, town, kingdom, age,
to darkness far deeper than that which fluffed
now at the neat new urinal's outline,
and heaved and beat behind it at the ruins.
Like a thud in the head, suddenly become memory,
stillness was dumb around me. Scrambling up
a heap of refuse, I grabbed at crystalled brick.
Flakes fell from my hand – a gruff tinkle –
no knowledge there of what brought the Hall low,
or concern either. Neither did I care.
Irrecoverably dead, slumped in rank weed
and billowy grass, it mouldered from here to now,
connoting nothing but where my anger stood
and grief enough to pull the sagging smoke down
from the sky, a silent, lethal, swaddling
over the garden I played in as a child,
and over those children – laughter in the branches –
shaking the pear-tree's last sour fruit to ground.

TONY CONNOR

Pollution. *Photo: Bruce Davidson*

St. Mark's, Cheetham Hill

Designed to dominate the district –
God being nothing if not large
and stern, melancholic from man's fall
(like Victoria widowed early) –
the church, its yard, were raised on a plateau
six feet above the surrounding green.
There weren't many houses then; Manchester
was a good walk away. I've seen
faded photographs : the church standing
amidst strolling gentry, as though
ready to sail for the Empire's farthest parts; –
the union jack at the tower's masthead
enough to quell upstart foreigners and natives.
But those were the early days. The city
began to gollop profits, burst
outward on all sides. Soon,
miles of the cheapest brick swaddled landmarks,
the church one. Chimes that had used to wake
workers in Whitefield, died in near streets.

From our house – a part of the parish –
St. Mark's is a turn right, a turn left,
and straight down Coke Street past the Horseshoe.
The raised graveyard – full these many years –
overlooks the junction of five streets;
pollarded plane trees round its edge,
the railings gone to help fight Hitler.
Adam Murray of New Galloway,
'Who much improved the spinning mule',
needs but a step from his tomb to peer in
at somebody's glittering television;
Harriet Pratt, 'A native of Derby',
might sate her judgement-hunger with chips
were she to rise and walk twenty yards.

The houses are that close. The church,
begrimed, an ugly irregular box
squatting above those who once filled it
with faith and praise, looks smaller now
than in those old pictures. Subdued
by a raincoat factory's bulk, the Kosher
Slaughter House next door, its dignity
is rare weddings, the Co-op hearse,
and hired cars full of elderly mourners.
The congregations are tiny these days;
few folk could tell you whether it's 'High' or 'Low';
the vicar's name, the times of services,
is specialized knowledge. And fear has gone;
the damp, psalmed, God of my childhood has gone.
Perhaps a boy delivering papers
in winter darkness before the birds wake,
keeps to Chapel Street's far side, for fear
some corpse interred at his ankle's depth
might shove a hand through the crumbling wall
and grab him in passing; but not for fear
of black religion – the blurred bulk
of God in drizzle and dirty mist,
or hooded with snow on his white throne
watching the sparrow fall.
                    Now, the graveyard,
its elegant wrought-ironwork wrenched,
carted away; its rhymed epitaphs,
urns of stone and ingenious scrolls,
chipped, tumbled, masked by weeds,
is used as a playground. Shouting children
Tiggy between the tombs.
                    On Saturdays
I walk there sometimes – through the drift
of jazz from open doors, the tide
of frying fish, and the groups of women
gossiping on their brushes – to see the church,
its God decamped, or dead, or daft
to all but the shrill hosannas of children

153

whose prayers are laughter, playing such parts
in rowdy games, you'd think it built
for no greater purpose, think its past
one long term of imprisonment.

There's little survives Authority's cant
that's not forgotten, written-off,
or misunderstood. The Methodist Chapel's
been bought by the Jews for a Synagogue;
Ukrainian Catholics have the Wesleyan's
sturdy structure built to outlast Rome –
and men of the district say St. Mark's
is part of a clearance area. Soon
it will be down as low as rubble
from every house that squeezed it round,
to bed a motorway and a new estate.
Or worse: repainted, pointed, primmed –
as becomes a unit in town-planners'
clever dreams of a healthy community –
will prosper in dignity and difference,
the gardened centre of new horizons.

Rather than this, I'd see it smashed,
and picture the final splendours of decay:
Opposing gangs in wild 'Relievo',
rushing down aisles and dusty pews
at which the houses look straight in
past broken wall; and late-night drunkards
stumbling their usual short-cut home
across uneven eulogies, fumbling
difficult flies to pour discomfort out
in comfortable shadows, in a nave
they praise with founts, and moonlit blooms of steam.

TONY CONNOR

Birches

When I see birches bend to left and right
Across the lines of straighter darker trees,
I like to think some boy's been swinging on them.
But swinging doesn't bend them down to stay
As ice-storms do. Often you must have seen them
Loaded with ice a sunny winter morning
After a rain. They click upon themselves
As the breeze rises, and turn many-coloured
As the stir cracks and crazes their enamel.
Soon the sun's warmth makes them shed their crystal shells
Shattering and avalanching on the snow-crust –
Such heaps of broken glass to sweep away
You'd think the inner dome of heaven had fallen.
They are dragged to the withered bracken by the load,
And they seem not to break; though once they are bowed
So low for long, they never right themselves:
You may see their trunks arching in the woods
Years afterwards, trailing their leaves on the ground
Like girls on hands and knees that throw their hair
Before them over their heads to dry in the sun.
But I was going to say when Truth broke in
With all her matter-of-fact about the ice-storm
I should prefer to have some boy bend them
As he went out and in to fetch the cows –
Some boy too far from town to learn basketball,
Whose only play was what he found himself,
Summer or winter, and could play alone.
One by one he subdued his father's trees
By riding them down over and over again
Until he took the stiffness out of them,
And not one but hung limp, not one was left
For him to conquer. He learned all there was
To learn about not launching out too soon
And so not carrying the tree away
Clear to the ground. He always kept his poise

To the top branches, climbing carefully
With the same pains you use to fill a cup
Up to the brim, and even above the brim.
Then he flung outward, feet first, with a swish,
Kicking his way down through the air to the ground.
So was I once myself a swinger of birches.
And so I dream of going back to be.
It's when I'm weary of considerations,
And life is too much like a pathless wood
Where your face burns and tickles with the cobwebs
Broken across it, and one eye is weeping
From a twig's having lashed across it open.
I'd like to get away from earth awhile
And then come back to it and begin over.
May no fate wilfully misunderstand me
And half grant what I wish and snatch me away
Not to return. Earth's the right place for love :
I don't know where it's likely to go better.
I'd like to go by climbing a birch tree,
And climb black branches up a snow-white trunk
Toward heaven till the tree could bear no more,
But dipped its top and set me down again.
That would be good both going and coming back.
One could do worse than be a swinger of birches.

ROBERT FROST

Slow-Burning Autumn

The silver birches are on fire
    With a thin gold flame;
The sharp leaves of the briar
    Burn with a russet gleam;
The bramble rough with red
    Is a smouldering ember,

And beeches though they soon will blaze
    As yet are amber.
Late apples like old planets rage
    In smoking air;
Their sheen with too great age
    Grows rough and sere
But still they do not fall
    Though the bitter quince
Already hangs full grown
    By the dry fence.

Grass like a lion's ochre mane
    Furs the hard earth;
In hedges down the lane
    Nuts swell in the sheath;
While in old gardens still
    The summer flowers;
Snapdragons by the flaking wall
    Raise up their spires.

Cornelian-bronze the pendent world
    Burns in a haze
Of thin mist whitely curled
    Like smoke under the trees:
Slow-burning autumn and
    Slow-going summer are one,
Deeply asleep, sharing
    The same gold dream.

JOHN SMITH

Autumn

I love to see, when leaves depart,
The clear anatomy arrive,
Winter, the paragon of art,
That kills all forms of life and feeling
Save what is pure and will survive.

Already now the clanging chains
Of geese are harnessed to the moon :
Stripped are the great sun-clouding planes :
And the dark pines, their own revealing,
Let in the needles of the noon.

Strained by the gale the olives whiten
Like hoary wrestlers bent with toil
And, with the vines, their branches lighten
To brim our vats where summer lingers
In the red froth and sun-gold oil.

Soon our hearth's reviving pyre
Their rotten stems will crumble up :
And like a ruby, panting fire,
The grape will redden on your fingers
Through the lit crystal of the cup.

ROY CAMPBELL

'Approach to the village', *Pissarro*]

Suburban Dream

Walking the suburbs in the afternoon
In summer when the idle doors stand open
    And the air flows through the rooms
    Fanning the curtain hems,

You wander through a cool elysium
Of women, schoolgirls, children, garden talks,
    With a schoolboy here and there
    Conning his history book.

The men are all away in offices,
Committee-rooms, laboratories, banks,
    Or pushing cotton goods
    In Wick or Ilfracombe.

The massed unanimous absence liberates
The light keys of the piano and sets free
    Chopin and everlasting youth,
    Now, with the masters gone.

And all things turn to images of peace,
The boy curled over his book, the young girl poised
    On the path as if beguiled
    By the silence of a wood.

It is a child's dream of a grown-up world.
But soon the brazen evening clocks will bring
    The tramp of feet and brisk
    Fanfare of motor horns
    And the masters come.

EDWIN MUIR

Jigsaws II

Property! Property! Let us extend
Soul and body without end :
A box to live in, with airs and graces,
A box on wheels that shows its paces,
A box that talks or that makes faces,
And curtains and fences as good as the neighbours'
To keep out the neighbours and keep us immured
Enjoying the cold canned fruit of our labours
In a sterilised cell, unshared, insured.

Property! Property! When will it end?
When will the Poltergeist ascend
Out of the sewer with chopper and squib
To burn the mink and the baby's bib
And cut the tattling wire to town
And smash all the plastics, clowning and clouting,
And stop all the boxes shouting and pouting
And wreck the house from the aerial down
And give these ingrown souls an outing?

LOUIS MACNEICE

Thistles

Against the rubber tongues of cows and the hoeing hands of men
Thistles spike the summer air
Or crackle open under a blue-black pressure.

Every one a revengeful burst
Of resurrection, a grasped fistful
Of splintered weapons and Icelandic frost thrust up

From the underground stain of a decayed Viking.
They are like pale hair and the gutturals of dialects.
Every one manages a plume of blood.

Then they grow grey, like men.
Mown down, it is a feud. Their sons appear,
Stiff with weapons, fighting back over the same ground.

TED HUGHES

Pennines in April

If this country were a sea (that is solid rock
Deeper than any sea) these hills heaving
Out of the east, mass behind mass, at this height
Hoisting heather and stones to the sky
Must burst upwards and topple into Lancashire.

Perhaps, as the earth turns, such ground-stresses
Do come rolling westward through the locked land.
Now, measuring the miles of silence
Your eye takes the strain: through

Landscapes gliding blue as water
Those barrellings of strength are heaving slowly and heave
To your feet and surf upwards
In a still, fiery air, hauling the imagination,
Carrying the larks upward.

TED HUGHES

163

[Aerial patterns at harvest time. *Photo: John Topham Ltd*

Mountain Limestone

Out of their shells the sea-beasts creep
    And eels un-reel from holes;
With eyes of stone they stare and weep
    Green stalactites of tears;
    On sea-washed caves of years
The temporal tide reclines and rolls,
And miser mussels, packed and pearled,
Lie like a clutch of peewit's eggs
    In the stone conger's coils,
    Looped around the world.

Where flimsy clints are scraped bone-bare
    A whale's ribs glint in the sun,
Coral has built bright islands there,
And birch and juniper fin the fell,
Dark as a trawling under-wave,
With rockrose opening three
Green hands that cup the flower,
And chiselled clean on stone
A spider-web of shell,
The thumb-print of the sea.
                NORMAN NICHOLSON

Discussion and Writing

1 Tony Connor's poem on p. 152 describes a building which has a special significance for him – St. Mark's Church. Perhaps there is a particular local landmark or area which you know well – a park, a church, a ruin, a monument, a radio mast – there are many possibilities here. Once you have chosen your subject try to capture its shape, colour and character in detail: if it has any special associations for you – maybe from years ago – include these in your poem.

2 In the speed of modern town life we tend to overlook the familiar and commonplace. Imagine the town area which you know best – perhaps your journey to and from school. Some of the following details are bound to stand out if you look at your mental picture carefully: lamp-standards, advertising hoardings, a group of shops or houses with a character of their own, gutters, a flyover, rooftops, neon lights. If there is a familiar sight or town landscape which you know well enough to describe in detail, you may find material for a poem.

3 Look at Pissarro's picture, *Approach to a Village* on p. 158. The end of the day atmosphere is created through the long shadows of the trees, the carthorse slowly plodding from the village, the air of stillness everywhere. It may remind you of a farm or village which you know – perhaps one you have visited on holiday. Either from your own memories or using the painting, try to create the slow, quiet atmosphere of village life.

4 Ted Hughes' poem *Thistles* on p. 163 focuses upon one small feature of the landscape but from it he develops several ideas and comparisons. Perhaps you could do the same. Use one of the following suggestions or, better still, find your own subject: a bird's nest; a field of grasses; buttercups or clover; a haystack; a particular tree – its shape, leaves and bark; a scarecrow; nettles.

5 Many people feel that one of the most unpleasant aspects of town life nowadays is the way in which city centres are choked with cars. Areas of many towns and cities suffer an almost permanent traffic flow, with a predictable jam at rush hours. Perhaps you could jot down words and phrases to describe the sounds, sights and smells of a traffic jam. How do drivers and pedestrians react? What are your thoughts and feelings as you watch hundreds of people, encased in their cars, all rushing home at the same time? There may be a poem here.

6 Look carefully at the photograph of harvesting in Kent on p. 164 and note down any details you find striking. Look, particularly for comparisons – what, for example, is the texture of the field like? Try to describe in a poem what you see.

7 The polluted stream in the picture on p. 150 is typical of the ways in which man destroys his environment. In what other ways do we do this? Can you think of any similar eyesores that you know in your own neighbourhood? Perhaps you can write about how this evidence of our 'civilisation' strikes you, either using the picture as a starting-point or taking your own line.

CREATURES

Humming-Bird

I can imagine, in some otherworld
Primeval-dumb, far back
In that most awful stillness, that only gasped and hummed,
Humming-birds raced down the avenues.

Before anything had a soul,
While life was a heave of Matter, half inanimate,
This little bit chipped off in brilliance
And went whizzing through the slow, vast, succulent stems.

I believe there were no flowers, then
In the world where the humming-bird flashed ahead of creation.
I believe he pierced the slow vegetable veins with his long beak.

Probably he was big
As mosses, and little lizards, they say were once big.
Probably he was a jabbing, terrifying monster.

We look at him through the wrong end of the long telescope of
  Time,
Luckily for us.

D. H. LAWRENCE

[Eggs hatching out. *Photo: courtesy of The Guardian*

The Dalliance of the Eagles

Skirting the river road, (my forenoon walk, my rest,)
Skyward in air a sudden muffled sound, the dalliance of the
    eagles,
The rushing amorous contact high in space together,
The clinching interlocking claws, a living, fierce, gyrating wheel,
Four beating wings, two beaks, a swirling mass tight grappling,
In tumbling turning clustered loops, straight downward falling,
Till o'er the river pois'd, the twain yet one, a moment's lull,
A motionless still balance in the air, then parting, talons loosing,
Upward again on slow-firm pinions slanting, their separate
    diverse flight,
She hers, he his, pursuing.

WALT WHITMAN

The Wild Swans at Coole

The trees are in their autumn beauty,
The woodland paths are dry,
Under the October twilight the water
Mirrors a still sky;
Upon the brimming water among the stones
Are nine-and-fifty swans.

The nineteenth autumn has come upon me
Since I first made my count;
I saw, before I had well finished,
All suddenly mount
And scatter wheeling in great broken rings
Upon their clamorous wings.

I have looked upon those brilliant creatures,
And now my heart is sore.
All's changed since I, hearing at twilight,
The first time on this shore,
The bell-beat of their wings above my head,
Trod with a lighter tread.

Unwearied still, lover by lover,
They paddle in the cold
Companionable streams or climb the air;
Their hearts have not grown old;
Passion or conquest, wander where they will,
Attend upon them still.

But now they drift upon the still water,
Mysterious, beautiful;
Among what rushes will they build,
By what lake's edge or pool
Delight men's eyes when I awake some day
To find they have flown away?

W. B. YEATS

Vulture

On ragged black sails
he soars hovering over
everything and death;
a blight in the eye
of the stunning sun

An acquisitive droop
of beak, head and neck
dangles, dully angling,
a sentient pendulum
next to his keeled chest.

His eyes peer, piously
bloodless and hooded,
far-sighted, blighting
grasses, trees, hill-passes,
stones, streams, bones – ah, bones –

with the tacky slack
of flesh adherent.
A slow ritual fold
of candid devil's palms
in blasphemous prayer –

the still wings sweep closed –
the hyaena of skies
plummets from the pulpit
of a tall boredom,
swallowing as he falls.

He brakes lazily
before his back breaks
to settle on two
creaky final wing-beats
flinging twin dust-winds.

He squats once fearfully.
Flushed with unhealthy plush
and pregustatory
satisfaction, head back,
he jumps lumpishly up.

Slack neck with the pecked
skin thinly shaking, he
sidles aside then stumps
his deliberate banker's
gait to the stinking meal.

DOUGLAS LIVINGSTONE

Snake

A snake came to my water-trough
On a hot, hot day, and I in pyjamas for the heat,
To drink there.

In the deep, strange-scented shade of the great dark carob-tree
I came down the steps with my pitcher
And must wait, must stand and wait, for there he was at
    the trough before me.

He reached down from a fissure in the earth-wall in the gloom
And trailed his yellow-brown slackness soft-bellied down,
    over the edge of the stone trough
And rested his throat upon the stone bottom,
And where the water had dripped from the tap, in a small
    clearness,
He sipped with his straight mouth,
Softly drank through his straight gums, into his slack long body,
Silently.

Someone was before me at my water-trough,
And I, like a second comer, waiting.

He lifted his head from his drinking, as cattle do,
And looked at me vaguely, as drinking cattle do,
And flickered his two-forked tongue from his lips, and
    mused a moment,
And stooped and drank a little more,
Being earth-brown, earth-golden from the burning bowels
    of the earth
On the day of Sicilian July, with Etna smoking.

The voice of my education said to me
He must be killed,
For in Sicily the black, black snakes are innocent, the gold
    are venomous.

And voices in me said, If you were a man
You would take a stick and break him now, and finish him off.

But must I confess how I liked him,
How glad I was that he had come like a guest in quiet, to drink
    at my water-trough
And depart peaceful, pacified, and thankless,
Into the burning bowels of this earth?

Was it cowardice, that I dared not kill him?
Was it perversity, that I longed to talk to him?
Was it humility, to feel so honoured?
I felt so honoured.

And yet those voices:
If you were not afraid, you would kill him!

And truly I was afraid, I was most afraid,
But even so, honoured still more
That he should seek my hospitality
From out the dark door of the secret earth.

He drank enough
And lifted his head, dreamily, as one who has drunken,
And flickered his tongue like a forked night on the air, so black;
Seeming to lick his lips,
And looked around like a god, unseeing, into the air,
And slowly turned his head,
And slowly, very slowly, as if thrice adream,
Proceeded to draw his slow length curving round
And climb again the broken bank of my wall-face.

And as he put his head into that dreadful hole,
And as he slowly drew up, snake-easing his shoulders, and
    entered farther,
A sort of horror, a sort of protest against his withdrawing
    into that horrid black hole,

Deliberately going into the blackness, and slowly drawing
    himself after,
Overcame me now his back was turned.

I looked round, I put down my pitcher,
I picked up a clumsy log
And threw it at the water-trough with a clatter.

I think it did not hit him,
But suddenly that part of him that was left behind convulsed
    in undignified haste,
Writhed like lightning, and was gone
Into the black hole, the earth-lipped fissure in the wall-front,
At which, in the intense still noon, I stared with fascination.

And immediately I regretted it.
I thought how paltry, how vulgar, what a mean act!
I despised myself and the voices of my accursed human
    education.

And I thought of the albatross,
And I wished he would come back, my snake.
For he seemed to me again like a king,
Like a king in exile, uncrowned in the underworld,
Now due to be crowned again.

And so, I missed my chance with one of the lords
Of life.
And I have something to expiate;
A pettiness.

D. H. LAWRENCE

Medallion

By the gate with star and moon
Worked into the peeled orange wood
The bronze snake lay in the sun

Inert as a shoelace; dead
But pliable still, his jaw
Unhinged and his grin crooked,

Tongue a rose-coloured arrow.
Over my hand I hung him.
His little vermilion eye

Ignited with a glassed flame
As I turned him in the light;
When I split a rock one time

The garnet bits burned like that.
Dust dulled his back to ochre
The way sun ruins a trout.

Yet his belly kept its fire
Going under the chainmail,
The old jewels smouldering there

In each opaque belly-scale :
Sunset looked at through milk glass.
And I saw white maggots coil

Thin as pins in the dark bruise
Where his innards bulged as if
He were digesting a mouse.

Knifelike, he was chaste enough,
Pure death's-metal. The yardman's
Flung brick perfected his laugh.

SYLVIA PLATH

Spider

Now, the spires of a privet fork from the hedge
And stretch a web between them;
The spider-nub eases his grip a trifle, twists a thread safe,
And the afternoon is quiet again.

Damp clouds drift above him; a burst of rain
Runs him back along a vane
To a leaf-shed, while it beads his web
And raises weed-smells from below
Of vetch, fumitory, and small mallow.

Hanging there are a dozen or so
Brown shells which tremble.
The curtain is ripped from the sun, and grass again
Leaps into its fumble :

Ants totter with their medicine balls and cabers, stone walls
Pop with their crickets;
A bluefly, furry as a dog, squares up
To the web and takes it with a jump like a hoop

And spider springs round like a man darting
To the fringes of a dogfight;

Tugging like a frantic sailor, buzzing like a jerky sawyer,
Fly finishes in swaddling
Tight as a knot
From the spinnerets' glistening.

And though spider
Hangs a little lower than the sun
Over all their heads, all
Seem ignorant of that passing;
The afternoon, the ebullience increases
Among the low boughs of the weeds
And spider steady like a lichened glove
Only a little lower than the sun; none
Takes account of that to and fro passing,
Or of the manner of that death in swaddling.

PETER REDGROVE

Second Glance at a Jaguar

Skinfull of bowls, he bowls them,
The hip going in and out of joint, dropping the spine
With the urgency of his hurry
Like a cat going along under thrown stones, under cover,
Glancing sideways, running
Under his spine. A terrible, stump-legged waddle
Like a thick Aztec disemboweller,
Club-swinging, trying to grind some square
Socket between his hind legs round,
Carrying his head like a brazier of spilling embers,
And the black bit of his mouth, he takes it
Between his back teeth, he has to wear his skin out,
He swipes a lap at the water-trough as he turns,
Swivelling the ball of his heel on the polished spot,
Showing his belly like a butterfly,
At every stride he has to turn a corner
In himself and correct it. His head
Is like the worn down stump of another whole jaguar,
His body is just the engine shoving it forward,
Lifting the air up and shoving on under,
The weight of his fangs hanging the mouth open,
Bottom jaw combing the ground. A gorged look,
Gangster, club-tail lumped along behind gracelessly,
He's wearing himself to heavy ovals,
Muttering some mantrah, some drum-song of murder
To keep his rage brightening, making his skin
Intolerable, spurred by the rosettes, the cain-brands,
Wearing the spots off from the inside,
Rounding some revenge. Going like a prayer-wheel,
The head dragging forward, the body keeping up,
The hind legs lagging. He coils, he flourishes
The blackjack tail as if looking for a target,
Hurrying through the underworld, soundless,

TED HUGHES

178

The Bull Moses

A hoist up and I could lean over
The upper edge of the high half-door,
My left foot ledged on the hinge, and look in at the byre's
Blaze of darkness : a sudden shut-eyed look
Backward into the head.

    Blackness is depth
Beyond star. But the warm weight of his breathing,
The ammoniac reek of his litter, the hotly-tongued
Mash of his cud, steamed against me.
Then, slowly, as onto the mind's eye –
The brow like masonry, the deep-keeled neck :
Something came up there onto the brink of the gulf,
Hadn't heard of the world, too deep in itself to be called to,
Stood in sleep. He would swing his muzzle at a fly
But the square of sky where I hung, shouting, waving,
Was nothing to him; nothing of our light
Found any reflection in him.

    Each dusk the farmer led him
Down to the pond to drink and smell the air,
And he took no pace but the farmer
Led him to take it, as if he knew nothing
Of the ages and continents of his fathers,
Shut, while he wombed, to a dark shed
And steps between his door and the duckpond;
The weight of the sun and the moon and the world
  hammered
To a ring of brass through his nostrils.

    He would raise
His streaming muzzle and look out over the meadows,
But the grasses whispered nothing awake, the fetch
Of the distance drew nothing to momentum
In the locked black of his powers. He came strolling
  gently back.

Paused neither towards the pig-pens on his right,
Nor towards the cow-byres on his left : something
Deliberate in his leisure, some beheld future
Founding in his quiet.

I kept the door wide,
Closed it after him and pushed the bolt.

TED HUGHES

The Outlaw

Kelly's kept an unlicensed bull, well away
From the road : you risked fine but had to pay

The normal fee if cows were serviced there.
Once I dragged a nervous Friesian on a tether

Down a lane of alder, shaggy with catkin,
Down to the shed the bull was kept in.

I gave old Kelly the clammy silver, though why
I could not guess. He grunted a curt 'Go by

Get up on that gate'. And from my lofty station
I watched the business-like conception.

The door, unbolted, whacked back against the wall.
The illegal sire fumbled from his stall

Unhurried as an old steam engine shunting.
He circled, snored and nosed. No hectic panting,

Just the unfussy ease of a good tradesman;
Then an awkward, unexpected jump, and

His knobbled forelegs straddling her flank,
He slammed life home, impassive as a tank,

Dropping off like a tipped-up load of sand.
'She'll do,' said Kelly and tapped his ash-plant

Across her hindquarters. 'If not, bring her back.'
I walked ahead of her, the rope now slack

While Kelly whooped and prodded his outlaw
Who, in his own time, resumed the dark, the straw.
                                        SEAMUS HEANEY

Bags of Meat

'Here's a fine bag of meat,'
    Said the master-auctioneer,
    As the timid, quivering steer,
    Starting a couple of feet
    At the prod of a drover's stick,
    And trotting lightly and quick,
    A ticket stuck on his rump,
Enters with a bewildered jump.

'Where he's lived lately, friends,
    I'd live till lifetime ends:
    They've a whole life everyday
    Down there in the Vale, have they!
    He'd be worth the money to kill
And give away Christmas for good-will.'

    'Now here's a heifer – worth more
    Than bid, were she bone-poor;
    Yet she's round as a barrel of beer';
'She's a plum,' said the second auctioneer.

'Now this young bull – for thirty pound?
    Worth that to manure your ground!'
'Or to stand,' chimed the second one,
    'And have his picter done!'

The beast was rapped on the horns and snout
　　To make him turn about.
'Well,' cried a buyer, 'another crown –
Since I've dragged here from Taunton Town!'

　　'That calf, she sucked three cows,
　　Which is not matched for bouse
　　In the nurseries of high life
By the first-born of a nobleman's wife!'
The stick falls, meaning, 'A true tale's told,'
On the buttock of the creature sold,
　　And the buyer leans over and snips
His mark on one of the animal's hips.

　　Each beast, when driven in,
Looks round at the ring of bidders there
With a much-amazed reproachful stare,
　　As at unnatural kin,
For bringing him to a sinister scene
So strange, unhomelike, hungry, mean;
　　A butcher, to kill out of hand,
　　And a farmer, to keep on the land;
One can fancy a tear runs down his face
When the butcher wins, and he's driven from the place.

THOMAS HARDY

Butchers at work. *Photo: Henri Cartier-Bresson*

Trout

Hangs, a fat gun-barrel,
deep under arched bridges
or slips like butter down
the throat of the river.

From depths smooth-skinned as plums
his muzzle gets bull's eye;
picks off grass-seed and moths
that vanish, torpedoed.

Where water unravels
over gravel-beds he
is fired from the shallows
white belly reporting

flat; darts like a tracer-
bullet back between stones
and is never burnt out.
A volley of cold blood

ramrodding the current.

SEAMUS HEANEY

Death of a Naturalist

All year the flax-dam festered in the heart
Of the townland; green and heavy headed
Flax had rotted there, weighted down by huge sods.
Daily it sweltered in the punishing sun.
Bubbles gargled delicately, bluebottles
Wove a strong gauze of sound around the smell.
There were dragon-flies, spotted butterflies,
But best of all was the warm thick slobber
Of frogspawn that grew like clotted water
In the shade of the banks. Here, every spring
I would fill jampotfuls of the jellied
Specks to range on window-sills at home,
On shelves at school, and wait and watch until
The fattening dots burst into nimble-
Swimming tadpoles. Miss Walls would tell us how
The daddy frog was called a bullfrog
And how he croaked and how the mammy frog
Laid hundreds of little eggs and this was
Frogspawn. You could tell the weather by frogs too
For they were yellow in the sun and brown
In rain.

Then one hot day when fields were rank
With cowdung in the grass the angry frogs
Invaded the flax-dam; I ducked through hedges
To a coarse croaking that I had not heard
Before. The air was thick with a bass chorus.
Right down the dam gross-bellied frogs were cocked
On sods; their loose necks pulsed like sails. Some hopped :
The slap and plop were obscene threats. Some sat
Poised like mud grenades, their blunt heads farting.
I sickened, turned, and ran. The great slime kings
Were gathered there for vengeance and I knew
That if I dipped my hand the spawn would clutch it.

SEAMUS HEANEY

185

Discussion and Writing

1 We often have curiously contradictory attitudes towards animals in that we are sentimentally attached to some and utterly repelled by others, yet it may be the ones we like that do most harm and those we dislike may not be only harmless but beneficial. It is perhaps worth considering how great the outcry against fox hunting would be if a fox was not a soft and furry creature but a slimy, fanged beast with three eyes.

Again, we tend to wax sentimental over lambs yet never shed a tear over a lamb chop. We find it difficult to think about eating animals and try hard to avoid thinking about the processes that bring the succulent steak to our table. Thomas Hardy's poem *Bags of Meat* is worth reading in connection with this. We often breed animals in order to improve the quality and quantity of their meat; we fatten them up on strictly controlled diets in confined spaces, sometimes in total darkness; we slaughter them and eat them. Perhaps after discussing some of the implications of these points you may find you are able to produce a piece of original writing on the subject. Factory farming, broiler houses, the slaughter-house are all topics worth thinking about. Why? The picture on p. 182 may help you.

2 Most of you will have visited a museum where there are collections of stuffed animals and birds, birds' eggs, butterflies neatly mounted in rows, the bones and skeletons of various creatures all carefully displayed for the interest of the public. Some of you may have visited a particularly large collection such as that of the Natural History Museum in London.

Think back to such a visit and try to write a poem about the atmosphere of the place, and your feelings about one or more of the displays.

3 You have probably used an aerosol spray against a fly or some other insect. Describe in detail what happened.

4 There is something very pleasing to people in the sight of animals grazing peacefully – sheep on a hillside, cows lazily munching their way across a field, horses at grass. Perhaps you could catch the atmosphere surrounding such a scene in a poem of your own.

5 Animals or birds often appear quite differently to us in winter

time and are usually more likely to be seen near our homes, looking for food and water. Try to write a poem about such a scene, being careful to concentrate on all the tiny details.

6 Because most people are town-dwellers and see animals as pets or in cages, the normal law of survival in the natural world – kill or be killed – tends to be forgotten. Birds of prey like Douglas Livingstone's *Vulture* (p. 171) or killers of the sea like sharks (which you may have seen on television in the films of Jacques Cousteau) may remind you that nature is still 'red in tooth and claw'; you may see in your own kitten or dog glimpses of the instinctive savagery of the tiger or the wolf. There may be an idea for a poem here.

7 Look carefully at the picture on p. 168. Try to imagine that you are actually watching the eggs hatching out before your eyes. Jot down quickly words, or phrases, ideas or comparisons to describe the following:

the markings on the eggs

the texture and appearance of the broken eggshells

the sense of fullness and weight of the unbroken egg

the size of the new-born bird against the egg

the bird's markings and feathers

the texture of the feathers against those of the nest and the rocks.

Aim to capture the details of the picture in words and you may be able to develop a poem from your notes.

POEMS TO COMPARE

A. End of the World

The world's end came as a small dot
    at the end of a sentence. Everyone died
without ado, and nobody cried
    enough to show the measure of it.

God said 'I do not love you', quite
    quietly, but with a final note;
it seemed the words caught in his throat,
    or else he stifled a yawn as the trite

phrase escaped his dust-enlivening lips.
    At least, there was no argument,
no softening tact, no lover's cant,
    but sudden vacuum, total eclipse

of sense and meaning. The world had gone
    and everything on it, except the lives
all of us had to live: the wives,
    children, clocks which ticked on,

unpaid bills, enormous power-blocks
    chock-full of arms demanding peace,
and the prayerful in a state of grace
    pouncing on bread and wine like hawks.
TONY CONNOR

The End of the World

Quite unexpectedly as Vasserot
The armless ambidextrian was lighting
A match between his great and second toe
And Ralph the lion was engaged in biting
The neck of Madame Sossman while the drum
Pointed, and Teeny was about to cough
In waltz-time swinging Jocko by the thumb –
Quite unexpectedly the top blew off:

And there, there overhead, there, there, hung over
Those thousands of white faces, those dazed eyes,
There in the starless dark, the poise, the hover,
There with vast wings across the cancelled skies,
There in the sudden blackness the black pall
Of nothing, nothing, nothing – nothing at all.

ARCHIBALD MCLEISH

B. Delight in Disorder

A sweet disorder in the dresse
Kindles in cloathes a wantonnesse :
A Lawne about the shoulders thrown
Into a fine distraction :
An erring Lace, which here and there
Enthralls the Crimson Stomacher :
A Cuffe neglectfull and thereby
Ribbands to flow confusedly :
A winning wave (deserving Note)
In the tempestuous petticote :
A carelesse shooe-string, in whose tye
I see a wilde civility :
Doe more bewitch me, than when Art
Is too precise in every part.

ROBERT HERRICK

Sweet Neglect

Still to be neat, still to be drest,
As you were going to a feast:
Still to be powdered, still perfumed:
Lady, it is to be presumed.
Though art's hid causes are not found,
All is not sweet, all is not sound.

Give me a look, give me a face
That makes simplicity a grace;
Robes loosely flowing, hair as free:
Such sweet neglect more taketh me,
Than all th'adulteries of art,
That strike mine eyes, but not my heart.

BEN JONSON

C. Early Morning Feed

The father darts out on the stairs
To listen to the keening
In the upper room, for a change of note
That signifies distress, to scotch disaster,
The kettle humming in the room behind.

He thinks, on tiptoe, ears a-strain,
The cool dawn rising like the moon:
'Must not appear and pick him up;
He mustn't think he has me springing
To his beck and call,'   .
The kettle rattling behind the kitchen door.

He has him springing
A-quiver on the landing –
For a distress-note, a change of key,
To gallop up the stairs to him
To take him up, light as a violin,
And stroke his back until he smiles.
He sidles in the kitchen
And pours his tea. . .

And again stands hearkening
For milk cracking the lungs.
There's a little panting,
A cough: the thumb's in: he'll sleep,
The cup of tea cooling on the kitchen table.

Can he go in now to his chair and think
Of the miracle of breath, pick up a book,
Ready at all times to take it at a run
And intervene between him and disaster,
Sipping his cold tea as the sun comes up?

He returns to bed
And feels like something, with the door ajar,
Crouched in the bracken, alert, with big eyes
For the hunter, death, disaster.

PETER REDGROVE

192

The Zulu Girl

When in the sun the hot red acres smoulder,
Down where the sweating gang its labour plies,
A girl flings down her hoe, and from her shoulder
Unslings her child tormented by the flies.

She takes him to a ring of shadow pooled
By thorn-trees: purpled with the blood of ticks,
While her sharp nails, in slow caresses ruled,
Prowl through his hair with sharp electric clicks,

His sleepy mouth plugged by the heavy nipple,
Tugs like a puppy, grunting as he feeds:
Through his frail nerves her own deep langours ripple
Like a broad river sighing through its reeds.

Yet in that drowsy stream his flesh imbibes
An old unquenched unsmotherable heat –
The curbed ferocity of beaten tribes,
The sullen dignity of their defeat.

Her body looms above him like a hill
Within whose shade a village lies at rest,
Or the first cloud so terrible and still
That bears the coming harvest in its breast.

ROY CAMPBELL

D. The Clod and the Pebble

'Love seeketh not itself to please,
Nor for itself hath any care,
But for another gives its ease,
And builds a Heaven in Hell's despair.'

So sung a little Clod of Clay,
Trodden with the cattle's feet,
But a Pebble of the brook
Warbled out these metres meet:

'Love seeketh only Self to please,
To bind another to its delight,
Joys in another's loss of ease,
And builds a Hell in Heaven's despite.'

WILLIAM BLAKE

Love

The difficult part of love
Is being selfish enough,
Is having the blind persistence
To upset someone's existence
Just for your own sake –
What cheek it must take.

And then the unselfish side –
Who can be satisfied
Putting someone else first,
So that you come off worst?
My life is for me :
As well deny gravity.

Yet, vicious or virtuous,
Love still suits most of us;
Only the bleeder who
Can't manage either view
Is ever wholly rebuffed –
And he can get stuffed.

PHILIP LARKIN

E. In Oak Terrace

Old and alone, she sits at nights,
nodding before the television.
The house is quiet now. She knits,
rises to put the kettle on,

watches a cowboy's killing, reads
the local Births and Deaths, and falls
asleep at 'Growing stock-piles of war-heads'.
A world that threatens worse ills

fades. She dreams of a life spent
in the one house : suffers again
poverty, sickness, abandonment,
a child's death, a brother's brain

melting to madness. Seventy years
of common trouble; the kettle sings.
At midnight she says her silly prayers,
and takes her teeth out, and collects her night-things.

TONY CONNOR

Love Songs in Age

She kept her songs, they took so little space,
  The covers pleased her :
One bleached from lying in a sunny place,
One marked in circles by a vase of water,
One mended, when a tidy fit had seized her,
  And coloured, by her daughter –
So they had waited, till in widowhood
She found them, looking for something else, and stood

Relearning how each frank submissive chord
  Had ushered in
Word after sprawling hyphenated word,
And the unfailing sense of being young
Spread out like a spring-woken tree, wherein
  That hidden freshness sung,
That certainty of time laid up in store
As when she played them first. But, even more,

The glare of that much-mentioned brilliance, love,
  Broke out, to show
Its bright incipience sailing above,
Still promising to solve, and satisfy,
And set unchangeably in order. So
  To pile them back, to cry,
Was hard, without lamely admitting how
It had not done so then, and could not now.

PHILIP LARKIN

F. Holy Sonnet

Batter my heart, three person'd God; for you
As yet but knocke, breathe, shine, and seeke to mend;
That I may rise, and stand, o'erthrow mee, 'and bend
Your force, to breake, blowe, burn and make me new.
I, like an usurpt towne, to'another due,
Labour to'admit you, but Oh, to no end,
Reason your viceroy in mee, mee should defend,
But is captiv'd, and proves weake or untrue.
Yet dearely'I love you, and would be lov'd faine,
But am betroth'd unto your enemie:
Divorce mee, 'untie, or breake that knot againe,
Take mee to you, imprison mee, for I
Except you'enthrall mee, never shall be free,
Nor ever chast, except you ravish mee.

JOHN DONNE

Thou Art Indeed Just, Lord

Thou art indeed just, Lord, if I contend
With thee; but, sir, so what I plead is just.
Why do sinners' ways prosper? and why must
Disappointment all I endeavour end?
    Wert thou my enemy, O thou my friend,
How wouldst thou worse, I wonder, than thou dost
Defeat, thwart me? Oh, the sots and thralls of lust
Do in spare hours more thrive than I that spend,
Sir, life upon thy cause. See, banks and brakes
Now, leavèd how thick! lacèd they are again
With fretty chervil, look, and fresh wind shakes
Them; birds build – but not I build; no, but strain,
Time's eunuch, and not breed one work that wakes.
Mine, O thou lord of life, send my roots rain.

GERARD MANLEY HOPKINS

G. The Pike

From shadows of rich oaks outpeer
The moss-green bastions of the weir,
Where the quick dipper forages
In elver-peopled crevices,
And a small runlet trickling down the sluice
Gossamer music tires not to unloose.

Else round the broad pool's hush
    Nothing stirs,
Unless sometime a straggling heifer crush
Through the thronged spinney where the pheasant whirs;
    Or martins in a flash
Come with wild mirth to dip their magical wings,
While in the shallow some doomed bulrush swings
At whose hid root the diver vole's teeth gnash.

And nigh this toppling reed, still as the dead
    The great pike lies, the murderous patriarch
    Watching the waterpit sheer-shelving dark,
Where through the plash his lithe bright vassals thread.

The rose-finned roach and bluish bream
And staring ruffe steal up the stream
Hard by their glutted tyrant, now
Still as a sunken bough.

He on the sandbank lies,
    Sunning himself long hours
With stony gorgon eyes:
    Westward the hot sun lowers.

Sudden the gray pike changes, and quivering poises for
        slaughter;
    Intense terror wakens around him, the shoals scud
        awry, but there chances

A chub unsuspecting; the prowling fins quicken, in
    fury he lances;
And the miller that opens the hatch stands amazed at the
    whirl in the water.

EDMUND BLUNDEN

Pike

Pike, three inches long, perfect
Pike in all part, green tigering the gold.
Killers from the egg: the malevolent aged grin.
They dance on the surface among the flies.

Or move, stunned by their own grandeur,
Over a bed of emerald, silhouette
Of submarine delicacy and horror.
A hundred feet long in their world.

In ponds, under the heat-struck lily pads –
Gloom of their stillness:
Logged on last year's black leaves, watching upwards.
Or hung in an amber cavern of weeds

The jaws' hooked clamp and fangs
Not to be changed at this date;
A life subdued to its instrument;
The gills kneading quietly, and the pectorals.

Three we kept behind glass,
Jungled in weed: three inches, four,
And four and a half: fed fry to them –
Suddenly there were two. Finally one

With a sag belly and the grin it was born with.
And indeed they spare nobody.
Two, six pounds each, over two feet long,
High and dry and dead in the willow-herb –

One jammed past its gills down the other's gullet:
The outside eye stared: as a vice locks –
The same iron in this eye
Though its film shrank in death.

A pond I fished, fifty yards across,
Whose lilies and muscular tench
Had outlasted every visible stone
Of the monastery that planted them –

Stilled legendary depth:
It was as deep as England. It held
Pike too immense to stir, so immense and old
That past nightfall I dared not cast

But silently cast and fished
With the hair frozen on my head
For what might move, for what eye might move.
The still splashes on the dark pond.

Owls hushing the floating woods
Frail on my ear against the dream
Darkness beneath night's darkness had freed,
That rose slowly towards me, watching.

TED   HUGHES

H. The Horses

I climbed through woods in the hour-before-dawn dark.
Evil air, a frost-making stillness,

Not a leaf, not a bird, –
A world cast in frost. I came out above the wood

Where my breath left tortuous statues in the iron light.
But the valleys were draining the darkness

Till the moorline – blackening dregs of the brightening grey –
Halved the sky ahead. And I saw the horses :

Huge in the dense grey – ten together –
Megalith-still. They breathed, making no move,

With draped manes and tilted hind-hooves,
Making no sound.

I passed : not one snorted or jerked its head.
Grey silent fragments

Of a grey silent world.

I listened in emptiness on the moor-ridge.
The curlew's tear turned its edge on the silence.

Slowly detail leafed from the darkness. Then the sun
Orange, red, red erupted

Silently, and splitting to its core tore and flung cloud,
Shook the gulf open, showed blue,

And the big planets hanging –.
I turned

Stumbling in the fever of a dream, down towards
The dark woods, from the kindling tops,

And came to the horses.
                        There, still they stood,
But now steaming and glistening under the flow of light,

Their draped stone manes, their tilted hind-hooves
Stirring under a thaw while all around them

The frost showed its fires. But still they made no sound.
Not one snorted or stamped

Their hung heads patient as the horizons,
High over valleys, in the red levelling rays –

In din of the crowded streets, going among the years, the faces,
May I still meet my memory in so lonely a place

Between the streams and the red clouds, hearing curlews,
Hearing the horizons endure.

                                        TED HUGHES

Horses on the Camargue

In the grey wastes of dread,
The haunt of shattered gulls where nothing moves
But in a shroud of silence like the dead,
I heard a sudden harmony of hooves,
And, turning, saw afar
A hundred snowy horses unconfined,
The silver runaways of Neptune's car
Racing, spray-curled, like waves before the wind.
Sons of the Mistral, fleet
As him whose strong gusts they love to flee,
Who shod the flying thunders on their feet
And plumed them with the snortings of the sea;

Theirs is no earthly breed
Who only haunt the verges of the earth
And only on the sea's salt herbage feed –
Surely the great white breakers gave them birth.
For when for years a slave,
A horse of the Camargue, in alien lands,
Should catch some far-off fragrance of the wave
Carried far inland from his native sands,
Many have told the tale
Of how in fury, foaming at the rein,
He hurls his rider; and with lifted tail,
With coal-red eyes and cataracting mane,
Heading his course for home,
Though sixty foreign leagues before him sweep,
Will never rest until he breathes the foam
And hears the native thunder of the deep.
But when the great gusts rise
And lash their anger on these arid coasts,
When the scared gulls career with mournful cries
And whirl across the wastes like driven ghosts:
When hail and fire converge,
The only souls to which they strike no pain
Are the white-crested fillies of the surge
And the white horses of the windy plain.
Then in their strength and pride
The stallions of the wilderness rejoice;
They feel their Master's trident in their side,
And high and shrill they answer to his voice.
With white tails smoking free,
Long streaming manes, and arching necks, they show
Their kinship to their sisters of the sea –
And forward hurl their thunderbolts of snow.
Still out of hardship bred,
Spirits of power and beauty and delight
Have ever on such frugal pastures fed
And loved to course with tempests through the night.

ROY CAMPBELL

Index of First Lines

Index of Authors

Sources and Acknowledgements

Thanks are due to the authors (or their executors), their representatives and publishers mentioned in the following list for their kind permission to reproduce copyright material:

W. H. Auden: 'As I Walked Out One Evening', 'Refugee Blues' and 'The Unknown Citizen' from *Collected Shorter Poems 1927–1957*, Faber & Faber Ltd.

Michael Baldwin: 'Death on a Live Wire' from *Death on a Live Wire and Other Poems*, Longman, by permission of the author.

Edmund Blunden: 'The Pike' from *Poems of Many Years*, Collins Sons and Co. Ltd. and reprinted by permission of A. D. Peters and Co.

Edwin Brock: 'Five Ways to Kill a Man' from *With Love from Judas*, Scorpion Press; 'Paternal Instruction' by permission of the author.

Alan Brownjohn: 'For My Son' from *Sandgrains on a Tray*, Macmillan & Co. Ltd.

Roy Campbell: 'Autumn', 'Horses on the Camargue' and 'The Zulu Girl' from *Collected Poems*, Faber & Faber Ltd, by permission of the estate of Roy Campbell.

Tony Connor: 'Child Half Asleep' from *Kon in Springtime*; 'In Oak Terrace' from *Lodgers*; 'End of the World', 'October in Clowes Park' and 'St Mark's Cheetham Hill' from *With Love Somehow*, Oxford University Press.

e. e. cummings: 'ygUDuh' from *Complete Poems 1936–1962*, MacGibbon & Kee Ltd.

Emily Dickinson: 'Because I Could Not Stop for Death' reprinted by permission of the publishers and trustees for Amherst College from Thomas H. Johnson, editor, *The Poems of Emily Dickinson*, Cambridge, Mass.; The Belknap Press of Harvard University Press, copyright 1951, 1955 by the President and Fellows of Harvard College.

Keith Douglas: 'Landscape with Figures' from *Collected Poems*, Faber & Faber Ltd.

Lawrence Ferlinghetti: 'At the Florist's' from *Selections from Paroles* copyright © 1947 Les Editions du Point du Jour, reprinted by permission of City Life Books; 'Sometime During Eternity' by permission of New Directions Publishing Corporation.

Robert Frost: 'After Apple Picking', 'Birches', 'Fire and Ice', 'Mending Wall' and 'Out, Out—' from *The Poetry of Robert Frost*, edited by Edward Connery Latham, Jonathan Cape Ltd and by permission of the estate of Robert Frost.

Bryan Guinness: 'What Are They Thinking' from *Reflections*, William Heinemann Ltd, by permission of the author.

Michael Hamburger: 'Paddington Canal' from *Flowering Cactus*, The Hand and Flower Press, by permission of the author.

Thomas Hardy: 'Bags of Meat', 'During Wind and Rain', 'Heredity', 'I Look Into My Glass' and 'Neutral Tones' from *The Collected Poems of Thomas Hardy*, Macmillan & Co. Ltd. and the trustees of the estate of Thomas Hardy.

Seamus Heaney: 'The Outlaw' and 'The Wife's Tale' from *Door into the Dark*; 'Death of a Naturalist', 'The Folk Singers', 'Mid-term Break', 'Twice Shy' and 'Trout' from *Death of a Naturalist*, Faber & Faber Ltd.

Phoebe Hesketh: 'Geriatric Ward' from *Prayer for the Sun*, Rupert Hart-Davis Ltd.

Miroslav Holub: 'Advent', 'The Forest' and 'Love' from *Selected Poems*, translated by Ian Milner and George Theiner, Penguin Books Ltd.

Ted Hughes: 'Second Glance at a Jaguar' and 'Thistles' from *Wodwo*; 'The Bull Moses', 'Pennines in April' and 'Pike' from *Lupercal*; 'Bayonet Charge' and 'The Horses' from *The Hawk in the Rain*, Faber & Faber Ltd.

Wole Soyinka: 'Telephone Conversation' from *Reflections*, African Universities Press, by permission of the author.

Jon Stallworthy: 'No Ordinary Sunday' from *Out of Bounds*, Oxford University Press; 'The Almond Tree' from *Root and Branch*, Chatto and Windus Ltd.

Dylan Thomas: 'Do Not Go Gentle' and 'Poem in October' from *Collected Poems*, J. M. Dent and Sons Ltd., and by permission of the Trustees of the Copyrights of the late Dylan Thomas.

John Updike: 'Seven Stanzas at Easter' from *Telephone Poles and Other Poems*, Andre Deutsch Ltd.

Arthur Waley: 'Plucking the Rushes' and 'A Protest in the Sixth Year of Ch'ien Fu' from *170 Chinese Poems*, Constable and Co. Ltd.

W. B. Yeats: 'He Wishes for the Cloths of Heaven', 'When You Are Old' and 'The Wild Swans at Coole' from *The Collected Poems of W. B. Yeats*, Macmillan & Co. Ltd. and by permission of Mr. M. B. Yeats.

Yevgeny Yevtushenko: 'Lies' from *Selected Poems*, translated by Robin Milner-Gulland and Peter Levi, Penguin Books Ltd.

The authors wish to thank the following for permission to reproduce the photographs:

National Gallery of Art, Washington, D.C., Samuel H. Cress Collection: 'Death and the Miser', Bosch.

The Mansell Collection: 'Knight, Death and the Devil', Dürer.

The Guardian and Robert Smithies: 'Gipsy Boys'.

Clichés Musées Nationaux: 'The Circus', Seurat; 'Approach to the Village', Pissarro.

Bill Brandt: 'Portrait of a Young Girl, Eaton Place'.

Gordon Newkirk Jr.: Coronal photograph from the 1970 Eclipse Expedition of the High Altitude Observatory, National Centre for Atmospheric Research, Boulder, Colorado.

Oslo Kommunes Kunstsamlinger, Munch-Museet: 'Attraction', Munch.

Imperial War Museum: 'A Dead German Outside his Dugout, Beaumont-Hamel, November, 1916'; 'First World War Recruiting Posters'.

Henry Moore: 'Atom Piece' and 'Rocking Chair No. 2'.

The John Hillelson Agency Ltd: 'Three Priests', 'Confrontation: Pentagon, Washington', 'Girl with a Doll, Washington', 'Pollution' and 'Butchers at Work'.

Philip Jones Griffiths and The Guardian: 'Youth Against the Bomb'.

The British Museum: Cartoon, Bruno Paul.

Fernand Léger Museum and SPADEM, Paris: 'The Builders', Léger.

Neville Cooper: 'Potter'.

John Topham Ltd and The Guardian: 'Aerial Patterns at Harvest Time.'

'Eggs Hatching Out' is reproduced by courtesy of *The Guardian*; we have been unable to trace the copyright holder.

We wish to thank our mother and our wives for the very considerable help they have given in the preparation of the typescript.

M.G.B.
P.B.